# ESSENTIAL POEMS & PROSE OF JULES LAFORGUE

# ESSENTIAL POEMS & PROSE OF JULES LAFORGUE

TRANSLATED WITH AN INTRODUCTION
by
## PATRICIA TERRY

FOREWORD
by
## HENRI PEYRE

BLACK
WIDOW
PRESS

Boston, Mass.

ESSENTIAL POEMS & PROSE OF JULES LAFORGUE

English translations © 2010 by Patricia Terry

Black Widow Press edition, October 2010

ISBN 978-0-98180885-7

Cover caricature of Jules Laforgue is by his brother Emile. (ca. 1875–80)
Dancing skeletons drawn by Jules Laforgue

Black Widow Press is an imprint of Commonwealth Books, Inc., Boston, MA. Distributed to the trade by NBN (National Book Network) throughout North America, Canada, and the U.K. All Black Widow Press books are printed on acid-free paper, and glued into bindings. Black Widow Press and its logo are registered trademarks of Commonwealth Books, Inc.

Joseph S. Phillips and Susan J. Wood, Ph.D, Publishers
www.blackwidowpress.com

Prepress production by Windhaven Press (www.windhaven.com)

10 9 8 7 6 5 4 3 2 1

# CONTENTS

# Foreword

O f all the "inheritors of unfulfilled renown," as Shelley in *Adonais* called poets prematurely dead, Jules Laforgue is the one who, in France, might have taken his place among the greatest. Unlike Rimbaud, he did not endeavor to change life through poetry and then renounce that magician's folly. Unlike Mallarmé, he did not pursue an Orphic explanation of this world in ever purer rhythms. The imperious genius of Rimbaud, the dazzling perfection of Mallarmé, have lately, in the eyes of posterity, dwarfed Laforgue to the rank of a minor poet. His compatriots have been unfair to him.

As an innovator, however, Laforgue is without peer in the Symbolist generation. What was most revolutionary in his colloquial language, in his use of irony, in his versification, has now been assimilated by the French, who can afford to be ungrateful to him. But without Laforgue, Guillaume Apollinaire, Jules Supervielle, Jean Giraudoux, Jean Anouilh, even Jacques Prévert might well never have come into their own. His inspiration has, more perhaps than that of any French poet except Verlaine, stimulated musical composers as diverse as Schonberg, Honegger, Milhaud, Ibert. Baudelaire and Rimbaud have posthumously been of disservice to both imitators and translators. Laforgue, hardly less of an innovator than they, more timid and resigned, has on the contrary fecundated such talents as were for a while possessed by him.

"A sort of possession by a stronger personality" is the phrase coined by T. S. Eliot to characterize the sway under which, for some years, Laforgue held the American poet. Eliot's debt to the French poet's themes, imagery, and rhythms is manifest in the four poems placed under the sign of

1

Laforgue, and also in *The Waste Land*. Alfred Prufrock, like the shy reader to the Empress Augusta of Germany, harried himself with the Hamletian question "Do I dare?" and "Do I dare?" and watches "the bald spot in the middle of his hair." He revels in the juxtaposition of unexpected images and in sneering at his own emotions. The "Portrait of a Lady" rings even more Laforguian, as do the repeated borrowings from colloquial speech inserted into Eliot's poetry elsewhere. Laforgue's fate seems to be to serve his purpose in other writers' development and, when transcended, to be discarded. Alain-Fournier, Eliot's French teacher in Paris, thus left Laforgue behind him after having cherished him. T. S. Eliot went much farther and deeper than Laforgue in his later verse, but he never totally renounced the French poet who first had shown him how to ring an original note in English poetry. In his Introduction to Ezra Pound's *Selected Poems* he acknowledged that he had drawn his form directly "from the study of Laforgue together with the later Elizabethan drama."

Ezra Pound followed suit and rejoiced in finding in Laforgue "that dance of the intellect among words." Allen Tate and Hart Crane also toyed for a time with Laforguian mannerisms and relived the spirit behind them. Indeed, no other French poet has enjoyed such a progeny in English-speaking lands, as Warren Ramsey has shown in his discriminating and perceptive volume, *Jules Laforgue and the Ironic Inheritance*. A British critic, less addicted to understatement than some of his countrymen, Martin Turnell, went so far as to decree that Laforgue's *Derniers Vers* constituted "the most important single poem published in Europe since the Seventeenth Century." The tough-minded Georgia lady who translated Laforgue's humorous prose *Hamlet* into English found it, *horrendum dicta,* "more profound than Shakespeare's."

A writer of such consequence in European poetry should be made available to those American readers who do not feel too sure of perceiving all the ironical or sentimental shades of Laforgue's verse. Fortunately, if it may be contended, as Malraux once did, that American literature is the first great literature composed by men who are not primarily intellectuals, such an assertion can only apply to novelists and short-story tellers. The critics and the poets of America rank among the most highly cultured men of the modern world. Wallace Stevens, Marianne Moore, Randall Jarrell, Richard Wilbur among the poets have been remarkably, almost dangerously, well informed on their French predecessors. Late in 1956, William Jay Smith brought out a version of Laforgue's *Selected Writings*.

Patricia Terry, Laforgue's present translator, is young, bold, and a very talented poet in her own right. Her French was perfected at Wellesley College, where it is taught in its subtlest nuances, and by a year's study at the Sorbonne. Her poetical gift was encouraged by one of the greatest poets of our age, the Spaniard Jorge Guillén, who might have been as expert with French verse as he was with Spanish, had he so chosen. Her rendering of the best of Laforgue was a slow labor of love. She has imbued herself with Laforgue's vocabulary, imagery, prosody. She has gone straightforwardly to the most difficult of Laforgue's poems: those which are pure music and those which may be called the "music of ideas," to borrow F. O. Matthiessen's phrase on T. S. Eliot. *Le Sanglot de la Terre* has the majesty of a cosmic sob, one of the least egocentric or anthropomorphic of the most philosophical wailings uttered in nineteenth-century poetry, which echoed with laments at the world's being wrong. The *Complaintes* show Laforgue's irony at its finest, as "the equilibrium of opposed impulses," in I. A. Richards' definition, a vengeance enacted against the platitudinous aimlessness of the world and of life, a subtle vindication of romantic love mocking itself. The *Derniers Vers* display Laforgue at his highest, maturing as an experimenter in metrics, as a liberator of French poetry from the stately Alexandrine, as a verbal inventor from whom Pound and Joyce were to borrow many a lesson. The selection here presented does full justice to the French poet's versatility.

The translation fulfils the primary requirement of any translation: it is faithful and, etymologically speaking, highly intelligent. It is doubly faithful because it is poetical. The qualities of Laforgue's torn, shy, seductive personality come through to the reader unimpeded by the language barrier. To be sure, a carping critic might take exception to this or that turn of English phrase. But the antinomy between perfect accuracy and a render-

ing of the poetical quality which lurks behind accuracy and at times seems
hostile to it is one which has tantalized every reader. A succinct foreword
should not indulge in cavilling at details when the rendering of Laforgue's
poetry offered here sparkles with talent as it does. May Jules Laforgue win
new admirers in this country, thanks to Patricia Terry's gifted and sedulous
devotion to the French poet!

—HENRI PEYRE

# Introduction

Oh! I was really struck by THIS LIFE OF MINE Last
Sunday . . .

The "good Breton" Jules Laforgue was born in Montevideo, Uruguay, on
August 16, 1860. When his father's small *lycée* failed, six years later, the
family moved back to France. Seventy-five days at sea provided Jules with
spectacular sunsets and an equally impressive boredom, prototype of the
ennui to come. Transplanted to Tarbes, Mme Laforgue and her five children
settled down for two years until Charles Laforgue returned to take all but
Jules and Emile back to Montevideo. Jules was a "dreamy . . . but remar—
kably intelligent" student (the principal's opinion) at the Collège Impérial
in Tarbes until 1876. He fell in love with "Marguerite," described in the
story "Amours de la quinzième année," a love violent, awkward, and from
afar, ending, according to the tale, with Marguerite's marriage to a "fat and
vulgar gentleman." Her shadow persists here and there among the poems.

By the time Charles and Pauline Laforgue returned from South America
in 1875, their family had been increased by five more children. Still another
was born that same year, and in 1876, shortly after they had all moved to
Paris, Mme Laforgue died giving birth to a twelfth child. Jules wrote later
that he had "hardly known his mother," and often, even in such graphically
unsentimental poems as the "Complaint of the Poet's Foetus," he reveals an
orphan's longing for the maternal consolations.

By 1879, Jules' artistic and philosophical, if not academic, talents had
earned him at least one literary companion, Gustave Kahn, who was in
some degree his mentor. Their conversations were soon interrupted by

Kahn's military service (Laforgue's health was already fragile enough to exempt him), and replaced by a correspondence which has been preserved. The letters tell us in particular about life in the Laforgues' Rue Berthollet apartment, the Sundays, overcrowded *en famille,* which became the leitmotif Sundays—tedious, chaotic, or simply melancholy. Jules also writes of religion, the undermining of what must have been a solid faith until he was nearly twenty. In one of his best early poems, a "pariah of the human family" observes Christmas Eve with a skeptic's nostalgia and pride.

To fill the vacuum left by departing God, Laforgue turned to a subjective idealism derived from Schopenhauer which led him through a period of ascetic renunciations and a "Buddhic suffering for all Nature, . . . meticulously, with all my nerves." A lasting result of this experiment was a vague and tormenting belief in the equation of chastity and truth. Another magnet was Eduard von Hartmann's *Philosophy of the Unconscious.* The title of that book referred not only to the submerged elements in the minds of individuals, but more particularly to an Absolute, itself unconscious, a cosmic principle having the characteristics of God minus the image of Man, and manifesting itself through the work of artists, "priests of the Unconscious," according to Laforgue. These metaphysical concerns are described in more deserving detail by Warren Ramsey in his *Jules Laforgue and the Ironic Inheritance,* to which I am indebted for much of this biographical information. The abstract concepts which are so noticeable in Laforgue's first book, *Le Sanglot de la Terre,* become increasingly less obtrusive until, dressed as clowns, they reappear in the *Moralités légendaires* to receive a final tribute of laughter at Herod's feast. But the acute questions to which they correspond remained vital. Laforgue's anguished need of a paradoxical purity—carnal purity, perhaps—was far from speculative; nor was his Absolute other than the Impossible, the infinite persistently crying to him from "out there," neither theoretical nor satisfying.

In 1881, when Charles Laforgue, already exhausted from illness and trying to provide for eleven children, returned to Tarbes, Jules was left in Paris to continue working for the art historian Charles Ephrussi. He was at that time dramatizing the results of his philosophical investigations in

*Le Sanglot de la Terre,* giving expression, generally inadequate or worse, to most of his permanent preoccupations. He quickly be came disgusted with its naive oratorical style and over-emphasized emotions, but one might well be more tolerant than he toward the obvious and fiery talent displayed in these poems.

The effect of uninhibited sincerity may be distrust. *Le Sanglot de la Terre* protests too much because Laforgue cannot see beyond his own emotions. It is only the truth which evokes his horrified revolt; later, when he has learned to embellish both sides of his dialogue with a veil of wit, neither cause nor response seems so exaggerated. A man who believes in death, and believes in it under the impact of revelation, might well throw himself on the ground and cry his despair to the stars with "How many days have I to live?" But a successful poem is not an expression of undistorted experience; not, in other words, life itself. It is experience presented obliquely, given a distinctive form which eludes the conflicts of personality to make direct communication possible. Once the poet relaxes his self-conscious grip on his subject and allows some apparently exterior consideration—the demands of a form, or even such a decision as Laforgue's "originality at any cost" to take hold, the true source of the poem may be illuminated by an alchemy that is partly dependent on the subconscious mind. Then the poem for both poet and reader is revelation as well as expression, and the problem which was its point of departure seems to be resolved rather than simply set forth.

The presence of death, the scientific vision of the Earth as "an atom where an ephemeral farce is played," Man as a uselessly miserable point between two blank infinities, the demand that Space give a sign of life— these are the major themes of *Le Sanglot de la Terre* and of the later books as well. If anything, this first presentation is the most optimistic. The organist's *miserere* will be so "cosmically desperate" that God *must* answer. And the skeptic on Christmas Eve still feels close enough to his renounced faith to be nostalgic. Philosophy seems to offer a remedy, or at least it guarantees validity to the artist. The poet's ambitions are not at all diminished by his revolt: if the earth is an aimlessly wandering dream, Laforgue can pass judgment on its history in eight stanzas, writing a funeral march for his own planet. This poem is the most successful of the series, Laforgue being obliged by his subject to put his own despairs in second place. Although the rapid enumeration becomes frenetic at times, its extraordinary condensation and the grave music of the refrain are unquestionable achievements.

Along with the "cosmic enigma" there is Woman, a problem even more hostile to solution. Here Laforgue doesn't go beyond a generalized condemnation ("the death rattles of the foul coupling of brutes") trying to harmonize with a compelling desire for love: "I might die tomorrow, and I've never loved. / My lips have never touched a woman's lips . . ." This is the source of his maturing paradox: Woman, who seems to be an invitation toward some kind of supra—terrestrial paradise, a virginal and superior reality, is in fact nature's most efficient device for enticing men toward the crudest of its requirements. Thus the alternating reproaches and longings, the hatred and admiration which Laforgue addressed to Her throughout his career.

The dedication of *Le Sanglot de la Terre* to Heine was more a prophecy than an indication of Laforgue's purposes at the time. The influence of Baudelaire is more apparent; some lines, "Voici venir le soir comme un vieillard lubrique," for example, seem to come directly from *Les Fleurs du Mal.* Ideas such as the "oasis of horror in a desert of ennui" must have made Baudelaire seem a companion in exile. No doubt Laforgue aspired to the sublime, but fortunately he wasted little time trying to walk in his predecessor's footsteps. If there are echoes later on ("O Nature, give me courage and strength enough / To believe myself old enough . . ."), they are used as indications of a well-established perspective, gestures of self-mockery in the direction of grandeur.

In 1881, thanks to Ephrussi and to his judiciously severe critic Paul Bourget, Laforgue was appointed reader to the Empress Augusta of Germany. Charles Laforgue died of tuberculosis shortly before the departure, but his son paid no farewell visit to Tarbes. His excuse for this is rather unconvincing, and perhaps he wished only to spare himself a painful and too late reunion. Although Laforgue has described his father as a man whom timidity had made hard, the poem depicting Ugolino who ate his children "in order not to deprive them of a father" suggests, as Warren Ramsey points out, a less affectionate understanding. Nevertheless, Jules had been very anxious for a farewell message from his father, and failed to receive one.

There followed five years of luxury, leisure, and boredom in Berlin, Baden-Baden, and Coblentz, following the fixed schedule of the court. Laforgue made few friends; one of them, the French journalist Theodore Lindenlaub, has described his rigidly masked shyness and uncertainties. There was, however, the young pianist Théophile Ysaye; "R," a woman attached to the court who engaged Laforgue in tempestuously futile duets; and at last the "petit personnage" Leah Lee from whom the poet took English lessons. Finding in her a sensitivity to match his own, he was able to imagine and finally to accept a precarious reconciliation with Woman.

He was at this time determined to leave the tedium of the court, although he was scarcely in a position to forfeit an adequate but fast-disappearing income. In September, 1886, having resigned in spite of the Empress' displeasure, he found the last-minute courage to ask Leah to marry him. The wedding ceremony in London the following December led not to the orderly work and emotional equilibrium Laforgue had expected, but rather to a struggle for life itself, first with economic realities, and then with the much more terrible practicalities of illness. In this last tormented year he nevertheless completed *Moralités légendaires,* those fantastic tales one of which, "Persée and Andromède" will be newly translated for this edition.

Laforgue's dialogue with death quickly assumed its final and expected form of coughing-fits and suffocations. Medical treatment, provided by Bourget, was apparently the best available, which did not prevent its being ignorant. Laforgue died of tuberculosis four days after his twenty-seventh birthday. Leah Laforgue died of the same disease only a year later. Although she did not have her husband's means for commenting on life, her hysterical laughter at his funeral is a terrifying postscript to the *(Oeuvres complètes.*

I have presented this capsule biography in order to provide a framework for a more detailed consideration of the poems. As Laforgue's route

between life and art was particularly direct, his readers may acquire much
biographical information once they are in possession of a basic outline.

It was in Germany in 1882 that Laforgue abandoned *Le Sanglot de la
Terre* for a totally different type of poem which he called a "complaint" in
reference to the folk-song style which provided its distinctive tone. In a let-
ter to his sister Marie he writes that he has discarded the heavy eloquence
of his philosophical poems. Finding himself more skeptical and less impul-
sive, possessing a more precise and "clownesque" technique, he is writing
little imaginative poems aspiring only to be original at any cost.

The volume, containing fifty Complaints, appeared in 1885, no fewer
than thirty-five of the poems having been written between November, 1882,
and August, 1883. In the verse prologue Laforgue looks back at the phi-
losopher of *Le Sanglot de la Terre* with a convert's astonished and mocking
fervor. No more black tears on Christmas ("Was it a dream?"), reproaches
to the "celestial Eternullity," "Buddhic suicides"—from now on he will be
vigorous, sentimental, down-to-earth. "Living is still the best we can do
down here."

The subject has not changed. Stripped of over-pretentious egocentric
statements, the "human cry" is still addressed to the great themes of love,
death, and the impossible. But Laforgue's refusals, personified in the sophis-
ticated melancholy of Pierrot, can now give birth to such a marvel of the
ironical love-duet as "She who is to put me in touch with Woman!" And
equipped with efficient verbal weapons, Pierrot deals with the Infinite:

> And I feel, having set my eyes
> On a life that's not to be realized,
> Less and less localized!

The King of Thule, guilty of no adolescent confusions, mourns carnal
metempsychoses and the death of a martyred sun. Woman, still a "chign-
oned mammal, false sister, false human," may yield "sexiprocal harvests."
And a bitterly humorous Science watches over the "subversive Microbe"
from foetus to death. True, originality at any cost, plus the extremely rapid

composition of the book, produced a number of undesirable inventions, awkward meters, unpleasantly eccentric rhymes, assorted exaggerations. Nevertheless, apart from the later free verse, the important stylistic elements which proved so attractive to Pound, Eliot, Supervielle, and others were already apparent. Laforgue had definitively found his personal perspective, his style, and had drawn from it poems to be placed among the best of his total work.

The two books composed almost simultaneously with the *Complaintes, L'Imitation de Notre-Dame la Lune* and *Des Fleurs de Bonne Volonté,* offer the most polished display of Laforgue's subtle or flamboyant virtuosity.

In the *Complaintes* the Moon had already triumphed over the Sun, henceforth to appear only in the melodramatic humiliation of its last moments. The *Imitation* is devoted to a celebration and explanation of this lunar superiority. The Moon is the country of suggestion where "Art is all . . . and its least glance / Is the infinite circle whose circumference is everywhere / And its immoral center nowhere" (a venerable phrase used by Rabelais to describe God, and by Pascal to define the physical universe). The value of suggestion as opposed to statement, the supremacy and also the sterility of art, are doctrines associated with Symbolism. But Laforgue's methods are as rigorously antisymbolic as his sense of humor.

Since these translations present little of the lunar natural history to which several poems of the *Imitation* are devoted, it might perhaps be summarized here. A landscape of pearl, ivory, porcelain, whose season is a perpetual autumn traversed by dolmen caravans, dotted with cemeteries. The inhabitants: sirens, sentinel toads, luminous sea-mammals, porcupines, pythons . . . and the Foetus grazing on ennui. The flowers: mandragora, cactus, hysterically smiling lilies. All this existing, for no particular reason, by virtue of an enchantment, and productive only of pure and absent-minded love. From another Laforgue perspective, the Moon is the wafer Host contained in a pyx of silence, reproach to human compromises with love and to our false humanizing of the cosmos. Pierrot, dandy of the Moon, says *amen* to the world while signaling toward the Absolute out of the corner of his eye.

Laforgue rejected *Des Fleurs de Bonne Volonté* as a whole, retaining only the poems which he retouched in composing *Le Concile féerique*. Parts of others found places among the *Derniers Vers*. Perhaps he objected to the lack of unity in the collection—certainly many of the individual poems are remarkable for their precise delicacy. Several familiar themes are given new clarifications:

> When I arrange a trip down into Me,
> I find, enjoying my good cheer,
> A rather mixed society
> That never passed my frontier.

There are further reproaches to women ("We are brothers!") for putting Man in the place of the Absolute. And "Soir de Fête" is an astonishing example of Laforgue's autodissection. Here the poet, having arrived at the end of a party because a beautiful evening went to his head, finds no one hurrying out to greet the prodigal, and retires in his gondola ("so frail!") to hide expectantly in the shadow of an arch. But left alone, he curses "this heart that wants me to be disdained."

In the *Faerie Council* Laforgue's talent for dialogue, already noticeable in the *Complaintes,* has created a short and philosophical drama. Some of the earlier versions indicated a dialogue form, but no participants were specified. Laforgue has turned away from the witticisms of Pierrot and the lunar landscape to consider terrestrial problems from a more relentlessly human viewpoint. The plot would be simplicity itself were the speeches of the Chorus not so uncompromising as to be occasionally obscure. A Lady and a Gentleman observe a starry night. The Gentleman makes a few disgruntled observations about the inhumanity of the cosmos and the pettiness of Earth. The Lady's enthusiasm for the cosmic spectacle is troubled by her fear of catching cold. Meanwhile the Chorus, having stated the moral:

> Hey! didn't decide
> To be born here, and men;

But now we've arrived
Let's stay till the end!

describes the scene from somewhere up above. Confused "tourists" are
seeking their route through multiple detours which lead back to the Lady
and the Gentleman now enjoying the "butcheries of love." There follows
a brief debate between Chorus and Echo on the merits of chastity versus
nature, interrupted by the Lady and Gentleman "dead drunk on ourselves"
who separate to declaim their opposing views about Woman. All partici-
pants reach the same conclusion, that of the "Complaint of the Incurable
Angel": Living is still the best we can do down here." To which the Chorus,
undeceived, adds: "Console yourselves, one and all."

At the very beginning of his career, Laforgue had imagined a poetic style
quite opposed to the nerve-taut nonchalance he then adopted. In a letter
of 1881 to Charles Henry (quoted by E. Greene, *T. S. Eliot et la France),*
he spoke of poems which would be psychology in dream form, inextricable
symphonies with a recurrent melodic phrase. This ambition was realized in
the free-verse poems written during 1886.

A particularly fine example is "Solo de Lune." Flexible metric patterns
evoke the variable rhythm of a stagecoach carrying the poet rapidly through
a moon-lit night. Superimposed on this, the rhythm of meditations center-
ing on memories ("ah! let's recapitulate") of a certain woman. We receive
only vague impressions of the absent heroine, frail, young, silently in love,
and, like the poet, guilty of not wanting to "take the first step." The story
is retold in a kind of day dream with various conclusions: a longing solici-
tude ("Oh! take care of yourself, at least, for me!"), rationalization ("But
even married wouldn't we some times groan, / If I had only known?"),
melancholies of solitude, and the final deftly ambiguous regret. This interior
journey back and forth through time merges with the traveler's immediate
impressions to form what is indeed an inextricably harmonized unity.

The Laforguian irony persisting in these poems is necessarily muted since
the free-verse form denies itself that concise mockery which is possible in
short rhymed stanzas. The themes themselves are more openly personal,

reaching that labyrinthine limit to introspection which prevented Hamlet, who appears so often in this volume, from telling his own whole story. The Grand Chancellor of Analysis is still pessimistically seeking some excuse for not letting the Earth "go out of season." But even more obsessive is the problem of chance-corrupted love ("If she had only met / A, B, C or D instead of Me . . ."), opposing his desire to accept, somehow, even the random offerings of fate since "sooner or later we'll be dead." Laforgue's attempts to weigh his desires against the facts, to live with open eyes, remain the source of his human cry at its most poignant and most complex.

Free verse has often been considered Laforgue's invention. Gustave Kahn claimed the honor for himself; Rimbaud has his own, more reliable, defenders. What matters to literary history is that Laforgue immediately understood the multiple requirements of free verse, that he succeeded in producing rhythms determined by the individual lines without sacrificing the larger rhythms of the whole; and that in spite of his own declared boredom with rhyme, he realized its value in preventing the free-verse poem from be coming excessively diffuse. The feeling of spontaneous inner monologue was achieved by skillful fragmentation of the subject, a technique that later was to be associated with Cubism. For these qualities Laforgue's last style was supremely important to the poets who looked to him for direction.

T. S. Eliot, Ezra Pound, Hart Crane, Alain-Fournier, and Supervielle have emphatically admitted their debt to Laforgue. Similar acknowledgments have been made on behalf of numerous other poets. His importance to American poetry in particular cannot be underestimated. Eliot's first book of poems, *Prufrock and Other Observations,* owes its very existence to Laforgue's magnetism. For Ezra Pound, Laforgue was "an angel with whom our modern poetic Jacob must struggle," and "perhaps the most sophisti cated of all the French poets." Laforgue's influence has been far too extensive even to be sketched in this brief Introduction. It has been possible only to indicate in the Notes the passages most conspicuously echoed.

Some statement of working principles should conclude a translator's introduction. I can locate only one. When direct circuits between the languages were closed, I have sought equivalents, even using totally different means toward what I hoped were similar ends. But radical departures from the text have not been necessary very often. Even Laforgue's humor is resistant to the usual sea-changes of translation for the very reasons which have often made him seem more foreign to his compatriots than to English and American writers. But no matter how favorable the terrain, translations are secondhand communication, and the translator must always look at least toward the poet with many regrets.

I am indebted to Mme Denise Alexandre of Brandeis University for the many hours before and after midnight she spent comparing Laforgue's French with my English, to Professor Otis Fellows of Columbia University for his critical reading of the Introduction, and to Professor Leroy Breunig of Barnard College for his valuable comments on the translations and the Notes. I wish also to thank Professor Peyre for his foreword, as well as for his early encouragement and skillful suggestions. Marguerita Howkins was of great help in the final proofreading.

I am happy to record my gratitude to Harold A. Small of the University of California Press. Many lines of verse in this book bear witness to his bilingual finesse.

My work on these translations was particularly favored by the constant interest of my husband, Dr. Robert Terry, who brings to the criticism of poetry his scientific respect for *le mot juste*.

—P.T.
New York, 1957

# Fifty Years Later

Laforgue was not the first poet I ever loved, but the first I ever tried to make my own, with the strange possessiveness of a translator. This was the beginning of a long series of such relationships each of which required its own language, and forsaking all others.

Much is said about fidelity to a text, and the various definitions of fidelity, but the translator seeks fidelity to her own reading and that, inevitably, changes over time. There may simply be the discovery of inaccuracies in interpreting the text—for example I may have been led astray by a natural inclination toward optimism, when, in 1957, I embarrassingly translated

> Le rêve
> C'est bon
> Quand on
> L'achève.

as: Dreams/ go wrong/ unless/ achieved.

But *achever*'s range of meaning is summarized in French-English dictionaries as finish (off.) It can mean to finish a speech or a project, or to kill someone. The lines that follow in the poem suggest that life is too short for a dream to be in any positive sense "finished." Nor would Laforgue's experience lead him to believe in such a possibility. Best, then, to get rid of it:

Dreams?
You win
When you do
Them in.

Since translation involves endless compromise, a more experienced trans-
lator may sacrifice a previously welcome rhyme for one less striking but
closer to what has come to seem the meaning:

For she was wed
To a certain gallant
With character
Instead of talent.

This now reads:

For she was wed
As they all saw fit:
He was rich and well bred—
No charm, no wit.

And then there are unnoticed confusions between French and English
pronunciation. For example, I had assumed that "Thulé" was spelled the
same way and pronounced "Tulay" in English. When something inspired me
to look it up, I discovered that the mysterious country is spelled "Thule" in
English and pronounced "Thulee." This required retranslation of the poem
"Complaint of the King of Thule."

Although I have made many changes in the English versions, I have
felt completely in agreement with my 1957 introduction to POEMS OF
JULES LAFORGUE. This is almost strange since I was much more like
him when I wrote it—just a few years older than he was when he died.
I too believed the Absolute more important than the Relative, that Love
should not be corrupted by Chance ("If she had only met/A, B, C or D/

instead of me . . . ") and in those years the landscapes of the Moon seemed
more alluring than those of the prosaic sun. Perhaps what has made this
poet part of my life for so long is the way he refuses to abandon his old
loyalties, but infuses them with an increasingly profound, and charitable,
self-knowledge. In one of his last poems he imagines his dream realized, but
a slightly lengthened line is enough to deflate it:

> Thus she would come, escaped, half-dead, to my door
> And roll on the mat I had just for that purpose put there.

Earlier he had fought off Reality with unique rhymes:

> Penser qu'on vivra jamais dans cet astre,
> Parfois me flanque un coup dans l'épigastre. (Clair de Lune)

(I enjoyed, and still enjoy, trying to find equivalents:

> That we live here on Earth with so much to vex us
> Strikes me like a blow in the solar plexus.)

But the opposite possibility: to win by submission, is sporadically, and
increasingly, apparent. The Pierrots say "l'art de tout est l'Ainsi soit-il"
("Let's say Amen, not make a fuss.") And the Chorus in "Le Concile Fée-
rique" replies to the Gentleman's bad-mouthing the Earth with:

> Hé pas choisi
> D'y naître, et hommes;
> Mais nous y sommes,
> Tenons-nous-y!

> Hey! didn't decide
> To be born here, and men;
> But now we've arrived.

Let's stay till the end!

My earlier reading noticed little reconciliation with Woman. I understood "Ces êtres-là sont adorables . . . " (Complainte sur Certains Ennuis) to be simply ironic. Now I see it could just as well be a kind of patronizing compliment, or perhaps a capitulation. Thus the earlier translation "Those creatures are adorable" now reads "Who said they aren't adorable?"

When not concerned with his personal hopes and fears, Laforgue's sympathy with the plight of women is intense. I notice this now much more than I used to do. Whether it's the orphan schoolgirl who in "Dimanches"

. . . threw herself into the stream -
No boatman, no Newfoundland dog to be seen . . .

or the victims of social conventions:

O immemorial slaves!
Oh! their little rooms
From which they are led down,
And down, and so they go
Toward domestic degradation -
No guardian angels here below.

And then, crossing their fingers, they say Amen,
In a passionless Suicide,
But attending to their own secret vows.

(Last Poems)

But Laforgue also protests that women, whether by inclination or in response to the expectations of their world, assume airs of superiority, trying to look like angels rather than human beings.

Let her adopt Man as her equal!

Oh! If her eyes could stop speaking of the Ideal
And content themselves with human affairs,
Like brother and sister at heart . . .                    ("Petition")

Despite the totally different style of its poems, the sound of Laforgue's
voice in Last Poems has not changed. It is a unique instrument capable of
expressing grief, mockery, self-deprecation, cosmic self-confidence, idealism,
hopelessness, and, increasingly, compassion. Only the greatest (arguably) of
all French poets, François Villon, had a voice with a similar range from
harshness to tenderness. And even he wrote nothing as touching as these
lines from "Simple Agonie:"

> . . . and even if we trample where we like
> Never will we be more cruel than life,
> Which makes there be animals unjustly beaten,
> And women ugly forever.

(In terms of translation, I have been told more than once that the phrase
"makes there be . . . " is awkward, even ugly, but my attempts at improving
it have only succeeded in weakening the statement. )

I omitted from the 1957 collection three poems from Last Poems, telling
myself they were less accomplished than the others. The truth is that having
set himself free from underlying meters, in these poems Laforgue plunges
into energies generated by the words themselves, sometimes straight into
incoherence:

> O diaphanous geraniums, warrior magic,
> Monomaniacal blasphemy!
> Delirium, debauchery, cold water! O a wine press
> For those great evening harvests!
> Layettes in distress
> Bacchantes in the forests!

This can make for uncomfortable reading, and even less comfortable translating. Themes, vaguely glimpsed, shift like the sequences of a dream. Juxtaposed to compassionate, hopeful, lines are stridently negative passages such as this:

> Truth from their lips?
> No! just hands on hips.
> From every one of them love comes your way,
> Simple and from the heart, like "have a good day!"

These poems are even more emphatic than the others of Last Poems in their preference for dissonance rather than compromise.

Even as he was writing his last poems, Laforgue was creating the unique prose of MORALITES LEGENDAIRES, here called LEGENDS AND MORALS. A translation of a story from that book, "Perseus and Androm-eda," has been included in this edition, an adventure which I would not myself have undertaken without the collaboration of Nancy Kline, a dear friend and a writer of such witty fiction that our combined efforts felt almost equal to the task. In any case it was highly enjoyable.

# from

## *LE SANGLOT DE LA TERRE*

# MARCHE FUNÈBRE
# POUR LA MORT DE LA TERRE

(Billet de faire-part)

*Lento.*


O convoi solennel des soleils magnifiques,
Nouez et dénouez vos vastes masses d'or,
Doucement, tristement, sur de graves musiques,
Menez le deuil très lent de votre sœur qui dort.

Les temps sont révolus! Morte à jamais, la Terre,
Après un dernier râle (où tremblait un sanglot!)
Dans le silence noir du calme sans écho,
Flotte ainsi qu'une épave énorme et solitaire.
Quel rêve! est-ce donc vrai? par la nuit emporté,
Tu n'es plus qu'un cercueil, bloc inerte et tragique:
Rappelle-toi pourtant! Oh! l'épopée unique! . . .
Non, dors, c'est bien fini, dors pour l'éternité.

O convoi solennel des soleils magnifiques . . .

Et pourtant souviens-toi, Terre, des premiers âges,
Alors que tu n'avais, dans le spleen des longs jours,
Que les pantoums du vent, la clameur des flots sourds,
Et les bruissements argentins des feuillages.
Mais l'être impur paraît! ce frêle révolté
De la sainte Maïa déchire les beaux voiles
Et le sanglot des temps jaillit vers les étoiles
Mais dors, c'est bien fini, dors pour l'éternité.

O convoi solennel des soleils magnifiques . . .

# FUNERAL MARCH
# FOR THE DEATH OF THE EARTH

(The honor of your presence is requested . . .)

*Lento.*

O vast convocation, magnificent suns,
Gather and loosen your masses of gold;
Lead tenderly, sadly, to solemn accords
The majestic funereal march of your sister, asleep.

Time has run out! The Earth, forever dead,
After a final gasp (where a sob trembled!)
Among the nocturnal silence of echoless calm,
Floats, an immense and solitary wreck.
That dream! swept away by the night, is it true?
You are only a coffin now, inert and tragic mass;
And yet remember! Oh, epic saga, unique! . . .
No, sleep; it's over now. Eternally, sleep.

O vast convocation, magnificent suns . . .

And yet, remember, Earth, that primal age
When you could summon through the monotonous days
Only the wind's pantoums, the muffled clamor of waves,
And silvery whispers among the leaves.
But the rebel, frail and impure, appears!
He plunders sacred Maya's beautiful veils,
And the sob of Time springs upward toward the stars . . .
But sleep; it's over now. Eternally, sleep.

O vast convocation, magnificent suns . . .

Oh, tu n'oublieras pas la nuit du moyen âge,
Où, dans l'affolement du glas du *Dies irae,*
La Famine pilait les vieux os déterrés
Pour la Peste gorgeant les charniers avec rage.
Souviens-toi de cette heure où l'homme épouvanté,
Sous le ciel sans espoir et têtu de la Grâce,
Clamait: Gloire au Très-Bon, et maudissait sa race!
Mais dors, c'est bien fini, dors pour l'éternité.

O convoi solennel des soleils magnifiques . . .

Hymnes! autels sanglants! ô sombres cathédrales,
Aux vitraux douleureux, dans les cloches, l'encens.
Et l'orgue déchaînant ses hosannahs puissants!
O cloîtres blancs perdus! pâles amours claustrales,
 . . . ce siècle hystérique où l'homme a tant douté,
Et s'est retrouvé seul, sans Justice, sans Père,
Roulant par l'inconnu, sur un bloc éphémère.
Mais dors, c'est bien fini, dors pour l'éternité.

O convoi solennel des soleils magnifiques . . .

Et les bûchers, les plombs! la torture! les bagnes!
Les hôpitaux de fous, les tours, les lupanars,
La vieille invention! la musique! les arts
Et la science! et la guerre engraissant la campagne!
Et le luxe! le spleen, l'amour, la charité!
La faim, la soif, l'alcool, dix mille maladies!
Oh! quel drame ont vécu ces cendres refroidies!
Mais dors, c'est bien fini, dors pour l'éternité.

O convoi solennel des soleils magnifiques . . .

Oh! can you forget the medieval night
When Terror would intone the *Dies irae*
While Famine ground up the old exhumed bones
For Plague whose fury gluts the charnel house!
Remember that hour when man in his ultimate fear,
Under the barren sky, still clinging to Grace,
Cried "Glory to God the Just," and cursed his race!
But sleep; it's over now. Eternally, sleep.

O vast convocation, magnificent suns . . .

Hymns! bleeding altars! O sorrowing jewels—
Windows of somber cathedrals, incense, bells.
And the organ unleashing powerful hosannahs!
O lost white cloisters! pallid claustral loves,
. . . hysterical epoch when greatly doubting man
Lost Justice and Father to find himself alone
On an ephemeral rock, careening through the unknown.
But sleep; it's over now. Eternally, sleep.

O vast convocation, magnificent suns . . .

And the stake! the irons! tortures! jails!
Bedlam and towers, brothels!
Alchemy! and music! and the arts!
Science! and war to fertilize the land!
And luxuries! black moods, love, and charity!
Hunger and thirst, drink, ten thousand ills!
Oh, what a drama you lived, fast-cooling ashes!
But sleep; it's over now. Eternally, sleep.

O vast convocation, magnificent suns . . .

Où donc est Çakia, cœur chaste et trop sublime,
Qui saigna pour tout être et dit la bonne Loi?
Et Jésus triste et doux qui douta de la Foi
Dont il avait vécu, dont il mourait victime?
Tous ceux qui sur l'énigme atroce ont sangloté?
Où, leurs livres, sans fond, ainsi que la démence?
Oh! que d'obscurs aussi saignèrent en silence! . . .
Mais dors, c'est bien fini, dors pour l'éternité . . .

O convoi solennel des soleils magnifiques . . .

Et plus rien! ô Vénus de marbre! eaux-fortes vaines!
Cerveau fou d'Hegel, doux refrains consolants!
Clochers brodés à jour et consumés d'élans.
Livres où l'homme mit d'inutiles victoires!
Tout ce qu'a la fureur de tes fils enfanté,
Tout ce qui fut ta fange et ta splendeur si brève,
O Terre, est maintenant comme un rêve, un grand rêve,
Va, dors, c'est bien fini, dors pour l'éternité.

O convoi solennel des soleils magnifiques . . .

Dors pour l'éternité, c'est fini, tu peux croire
Que ce drame inouï ne fut qu'un cauchemar,
Tu n'est plus qu'un tombeau qui promène au hasard
   . . . sans nom dans le noir sans mémoire.
C'était un songe, oh! oui, tu n'as jamais été!
Tout est seul! nul témoin! rien ne voit, rien ne pense.
Il n'y a que le noir, le temps et le silence . . .
Dors, tu viens de rêver, dors pour l'éternité.

O convoi solennel des soleils magnifiques,
Nouez et dénouez vos vastes masses d'or,
Doucement, tristement, sur de graves musiques,
Menez le deuil très lent de votre sœur qui dort.

Where is Buddha now, chaste heart and too sublime,
Who bled for the world and spoke the worthy Law?
And Jesus, sad and gentle, who doubted the Faith
By which he had lived, whose victim at last he died?
All those tormented by the atrocious quest,
Their madness, their books' unfathomed emptiness?
And all the unknown and humble who silently bled! . . .
But sleep; it's over now. Eternally, sleep.

O vast convocation, magnificent suns . . .

And nothing remains! O marble Venus, vain etchings!
Insane Hegelian brain! sweet consoling songs!
Belfries of filigree woven, upspringing, consumed!
Books which held man's useless victories!
All that was born of your children's wrath,
All that was once your filth and your transient splendor,
O Earth, has become like a dream, a noble dream.
Go to sleep; it's over now. Eternally, sleep.

O vast convocation, magnificent suns . . .

Eternally sleep; it's done. Believe if you will
The whole fantastic drama an evil dream.
You have become a tomb which aimlessly wanders
. . . nameless within the unremembering darkness.
It *was* a dream! It's true! you never lived!
All is alone! no witness! nothing to see or to think.
Nothing but darkness, time, and the silence . . .
Sleep; you've been dreaming. Eternally, sleep.

O vast convocation, magnificent suns,
Gather and loosen your masses of gold;
Lead tenderly, sadly, to solemn accords
The majestic funereal march of your sister, asleep.

# from

## *LES COMPLAINTES*

# COMPLAINTE
## DE LA BONNE DÉFUNTE

Elle fuyait par l'avenue;
Je la suivais illuminé.
Ses yeux disaient: "J'ai deviné
Hélas! que tu m'as reconnue!"

Je la suivis illuminé!
Yeux désolés, bouche ingénue,
Pourquoi l'avais-je reconnue,
Elle, loyal rêve mort-né?

Yeux trop mûrs, mais bouche ingénue;
Œillet blanc, d'azur trop veiné;
Oh! oui, rien qu'un rêve mort-né,
Car, défunte elle est devenue.

Gis, œillet, d'azur trop veiné,
La vie humaine continue
Sans toi, défunte devenue.
Oh! je rentrerai sans dîner!

Vrai, je ne l'ai jamais connue.

# COMPLAINT
## ABOUT A LADY GOOD AND DEAD

She fled along the avenue;
I followed, magnetized!
Her eyes were saying, "Alas, I knew
You recognized me too!"

I followed, magnetized!
Ingenuous mouth, regretful eyes;
Oh, why did I recognize
That loyal stillborn dream of you?

Lips so pure, but old her eyes;
A white carnation veined too blue!
Oh, nothing, of course, but a stillborn prize,
Far too dead to be true.

Sleep, carnation veined too blue,
Human life somehow survives
Without, defunct now, you.
I'll fast at home for this surprise!

True, she was no one I knew.

## COMPLAINTE
## D'UN CERTAIN DIMANCHE

Elle ne concevait pas qu'aimer fût l'ennemi d'aimer.
Sainte-Beuve, *Volupté*


L'homme n'est pas méchant, ni la femme éphémère.
Ah! fous dont au casino battent les talons,
Tout homme pleure un jour et toute femme est mère,
          Nous sommes tous filials, allons!
Mais quoi! les Destins ont des partis pris si tristes,
Qui font que, les uns loin des autres, l'on s'exile,
Qu'on se traite à tort et à travers d'égoïstes,
Et qu'on s'use à trouver quelque unique Évangile.
Ah! jusqu'à ce que la nature soit bien bonne,
          Moi je veux vivre monotone.


Dans ce village en falaises, loin, vers les cloches,
Je redescends dévisagé par les enfants
Qui s'en vont faire bénir de tièdes brioches;
          Et rentré, mon sacré-cœur se fend!
Les moineaux des vieux toits pépient à ma fenêtre.
Ils me regardent dîner, sans faim, à la carte;
Des âmes d'amis morts les habitent peut-être?
Je leur jette du pain: comme blessés, ils partent!
Ah! jusqu'à ce que la nature soit bien bonne,
          Moi je veux vivre monotone.


Elle est partie hier. Suis-je pas triste d'elle?
Mais c'est vrai! Voilà donc le fond de mon chagrin!
Oh! ma vie est aux plis de ta jupe fidèle!
          Son mouchoir me flottait sur le Rhin
Seul. Le Couchant retient un moment son Quadrige
En rayons où le ballet des moucherons danse,

## COMPLAINT
## ABOUT A CERTAIN SUNDAY

> She didn't understand that love was the enemy of love.
>
> Sainte-Beuve, *Volupté*

Man isn't really so bad, nor woman ephemeral.
Ah! fools cooling your heels at the casino,
All men weep one day, and every woman's maternal;
      Everything's filial, you know!
It's only that Fates employ such sorry prejudice
To make us, far and separate, self-exiles,
And blindly calling each other egotists,
And worn out with looking for some unique Anodyne.
Ah! until nature has pity on us,
      I'll take my life monotonous.

In this distant cliff-bound village, toward the bells
Once again I come down, through the piercing stares
Of children out for blessings on warm rolls;
      And then, at home, my wretched heart despairs.
The old roof's sparrows chirping at my window
Watch me eat, without appetite, à *la carte;*
Perhaps they house my dead friends' souls?
I throw them some bread; as if wounded, they depart!
Ah! until nature has pity on us,
      I'll take my life monotonous.

She left yesterday. Perhaps I mind?
Ah yes! So that's what hurts!
My life is caught among your faithful skirts!
      Her handkerchief swept me along the Rhine . . .
Alone. The Sunset holds back its Chariot's prancing
In rays where the midges' ballet is dancing,

Puis, vers les toits fumants de la soupe, il s'afflige . . .
Et c'est le Soir, l'insaisissable confidence . . .
Ah! jusqu'à ce que la nature soit bien bonne,
        Faudra-t-il vivre monotone?

Que d'yeux, en éventail, en ogive, ou d'inceste,
Depuis que l'Etre espère, ont réclamé leurs droits!
O ciels, les yeux pourrissent-ils comme le reste?
        Oh! qu'il fait seul! oh! fait-il froid!
Oh, que d'après-midi d'automne à vivre encore!
Le Spleen, eunuque à froid, sur nos rêves se vautre!
Or, ne pouvant redevenir des madrépores,
O mes humains, consolons-nous les uns les autres.
Et jusqu'à ce que la nature soit bien bonne,
        Tâchons de vivre monotone.

*Coblentz. Juillet 1883.*

Then, toward the soup-smoking roofs, it complains . . .
And evening so elusively explains . . .
Ah! until nature has pity on us,
      Must life be so monotonous?

Fans, pointed arches, or incestuous—how many eyes,
Since Being first had hopes, have demanded their rights!
O skies, will the eyes decay like the rest?
      Oh, alone! alone! and so cold!
How many Fall afternoons can life digest?
Ennui, cold eunuch, sprawls all over our dreams!
So, since we'll never be madrepores again,
We'd better console each other, my fellow men.
And, until nature has pity on us,
      Let's try to live monotonous.

*Coblentz, July 1883.*

## COMPLAINTE
## DU FOETUS DU POÈTE

Blasé, dis-je! En avant,
Déchirer la nuit gluante des racines,
A travers maman, amour tout d'albumine,
Vers le plus clair! vers l'alme et riche étamine
    D'un soleil levant!

—Chacun son tour, il est temps que je m'émancipe,
Irradiant des Limbes mon inédit type!

    En avant!
Sauvé des steppes du mucus, à la nage
Téter soleil! et soûl de lait d'or, bavant,
Dodo à les seins dorloteurs des nuages,
    Voyageurs savants!

—A rêve que veux-tu, là-bas, je vivrai dupe
D'une âme en coup de vent dans la fraîcheur des jupes!

    En avant!
Dodo sur le lait caillé des bons nuages
Dans la main de Dieu, bleue, aux mille yeux vivants
Au pays du vin viril faire naufrage!
    Courage,
    Là, là, je me dégage . . .

—Et je communierai, le front vers l'Orient,
Sous les espèces des baisers inconscients!

    En avant!
Cogne, glas des nuits! filtre, soleil solide!
Adieu, forêts d'aquarium qui, me couvant,

# COMPLAINT
# OF THE POET'S FOETUS

Blasé, I say! Go on,
Rip this sticky-rooted night
Straight across mother's all-albuminous love
Toward the light's nutricious stamens there above,
   A rising sun!

Each in his turn! It's time that I break free,
Shining forth from Limbo the one and only Me!

   Go on!
Saved from the mucus steppes, afloat,
Suckle the sun! then drooling-drunk on milk of gold,
Sleepyhead on the lulling breasts of clouds
    Wise and on the run!

—Ideal, of course; down there I'll play the fool,
Safe among shadowy skirts, to a wind-blown soul!

   Go on!
Sleepyhead on the clotted milk of skies,
The hand of God, blue, with a thousand living eyes,
Then shipwreck in the land of virile wine!
    Act your age!
    Just disengage . . .

Bowed toward the Orient's promises,
I'll take communion via unconscious kisses.

   Go on!
Sound off, gong of nights! Come in, solid sun!
Farewell, aquarium forests, warming gloom,

Avez mis ce levain dans ma chrysalide!
Mais j'ai froid! En avant!
Ah! maman . . .

Vous, Madame, allaitez le plus longtemps possible
Et du plus Seul de vous ce pauvre enfant-terrible.

You dropped this yeast into my tight cocoon!
But I'm cold! Go on!
Ah! *maman* . . .

From your Solitude, as long as possible, nurse,
Madam, this prodigy for better or worse.

## COMPLAINTE DE LA LUNE
## EN PROVINCE

Ah! la belle pleine Lune,
Grosse comme une fortune!

La retraite sonne au loin,
Un passant, monsieur l'adjoint;

Un clavecin joue en face,
Un chat traverse la place:

La province qui s'endort!
Plaquant un dernier accord,

Le piano clôt sa fenêtre.
Quelle heure peut-il bien être?

Calme Lune, quel exil!
Faut-il dire: ainsi soit-il?

Lune, ô dilettante Lune,
A tous les climats commune,

Tu vis hier le Missouri,
Et les remparts de Paris,

Les fiords bleus de la Norvège,
Les pôles, les mers, que sais-je?

Lune heureuse! ainsi tu vois,
A cette heure, le convoi

De son voyage de noce!
Ils sont partis pour l'Ecosse.

# COMPLAINT OF THE MOON
# IN THE COUNTRY

Ah! the Moon's grown old,
Fat as a sack of gold!

Retreat from afar vibrates,
A passing magistrate;

A harpsichord plays over there,
A cat crosses the square;

To the country, closing its eyes!
A final chord replies,

The piano closes its window.
What time can it be now?

Peaceful Moon, to this exile
Must I say amen, and smile?

O dilettante Moon, far or near,
There's nowhere you do not appear.

You saw the Missouri yesterday,
And Parisian ramparts, far away.

The blue fiords of Norway,
The poles, the seas—what else to say?

Happy Moon, and so you scan
At this hour the caravan

Of her wedding trip! I understand
A trip to Scotland's what they planned.

Quel panneau, si, cet hiver,
Elle eût pris au mot mes vers!

Lune, vagabonde Lune,
Faisons cause et mœurs communes?

O riches nuits! je me meurs,
La province dans le cœur!

Et la lune a, bonne vieille,
Du coton dans les oreilles.

*Cassel. Juillet 1884.*

Just last winter—how absurd
If she took my verses at their word!

O Moon, Moon, you vagabond,
Can we live faithful to our bond?

From my life, it seems, I'll soon depart,
But this countryside won't leave my heart.

And the Moon, that good old lady, wears
Cotton in her ears.

*Cassel, July 1884.*

## COMPLAINTE
## DE LORD PIERROT

Au clair de la lune,
Mon ami Pierrot,
Filons, en costume,
Présider là-haut!
Ma cervelle est morte.
Que le Christ l'emporte!
Béons à la Lune,
La bouche en zéro.

Inconscient, descendez en nous par réflexes:
Brouillez les cartes, les dictionnaires, les sexes.
Tournons d'abord sur nous-même, comme un fakir!
(Agiter le pauvre être, avant de s'en servir.)

J'ai le cœur chaste et vrai comme une bonne lampe;
Oui, je suis en taille-douce, comme une estampe.

Vénus, énorme comme le Régent,
Déjà se pâme à l'horizon des grèves;
Et c'est l'heure, ô gens nés casés, bonnes gens,
De s'étourdir en longs trilles de rêves!
Corybanthe, aux quatre vents tous les draps!
Disloque tes pudeurs, à bas les lignes!
En costume blanc, je ferai le cygne,
Après nous le Déluge, ô ma Léda!
Jusqu'à ce que tournent tes yeux vitreux,
Que tu grelottes en rires affreux,
Hop! enlevons sur les horizons fades
Les menuets de nos pantalonnades!
    Tiens! l'Univers
    Est à l'envers . . .

# COMPLAINT
# OF LORD PIERROT

*Au clair de la lune,*
*Mon ami Pierrot,*
Up to the skies, let's go,
Dressed to direct the Show!
Now my brain's quite dead,
To Christ be it sped!
Let's bay at the Moon,
Our mouths shaped like O.

Unconscious, descend into us by reflexes;
Shuffle the cards, the dictionaries, sexes.
First, let's whirl around like a dervish musing!
(Shake the poor being well before using.)

Like a good lamp, my heart is honest and well-behaved,
Yes, just like a print, I am most delicately engraved.

Venus, as large as the Jubilee,
Swoons already on the horizon hills;
It's time, good folks, to forget about destiny,
And drown your sorrows in long dreaming trills!
Your drapes to the four winds, Corybant!
Dislodge your modesty, down with your lines!
In my white costume, the swan part's mine,
O my Leda, and after us the Deluge!
Until, rolling your vitreous eyes,
You shiver in horrible laughing cascades,
Up! Let's plant against colorless skies
The minuets of our masquerades!
Oh, look! the universe
Is in reverse . . .

—Tout cela vous honore,
Lord Pierrot, mais encore?

Ah! qu'une, d'elle-même, un beau soir sût venir,
Ne voyant que boire à mes lèvres, ou mourir!

Je serais, savez-vous, la plus noble conquête
Que femme, au plus ravi du Rêve, eût jamais faite!

D'ici-là, qu'il me soit permis
De vivre de vieux compromis.

Où commence, où finit l'humaine
Ou la divine dignité?

Jonglons avec les entités,
Pierrot s'agite et Tout le mène!
Laissez faire, laissez passer;
Laissez passer, et laisser faire;
Le semblable, c'est le contraire,

Et l'univers, c'est pas assez!
Et je me sens, ayant pour cible
Adopté la vie impossible,
De moins en moins localisé!

    —Tout cela vous honore,
     Lord Pierrot, mais encore?

—Il faisait, ah! si chaud, si sec.
Voici qu'il pleut, qu'il pleut, bergères!
Les pauvres Vénus bocagères
Ont la roupie à leur nez grec!

—For that, take a bow,
Lord Pierrot, and now?

—Ah, if one of them, some fine evening would try -
Blind but to drink at my lips, or die!

I would be, don't you know, the noblest conquest
That woman at summits of Dream has ever possessed!

Until then, let none of you criticize
If I live by the ancient compromise.

Where begins or ends divine
Or human dignity?

Let's juggle with the entities;
Pierrot stirs, but follows All!
Let it be, let it pass;
Let it pass, let it be;
Similars are contraries,

And the universe, that's not enough!
And I feel, having set my eyes
On a life that's not to be realized,
Less and less localized!

—For that, take a bow,
Lord Pierrot, and now?

—The weather was, ah! so hot and dry.
And now it's raining, raining on the roses!
And all the poor Venuses in the grove
Have smut on their Greek noses!

—Oh! de moins en moins drôle;
Pierrot sait mal son rôle?

—J'ai le cœur triste comme un lampion forain . . .
Bah! j'irai passer la nuit dans le premier train;

Sûr d'aller, ma vie entière,
Malheureux comme les pierres. (*Bis.*)

—Oh, it gets less and less droll;
Doesn't Pierrot know his role?

—Dull as a carnaval lamp is my brain . . .
Bah! I'll go spend the night in a train;

Sure of spending my life alone,
Unhappily, since Pierre is stone. (*Bis.*)

## AUTRE COMPLAINTE
## DE LORD PIERROT

Celle qui doit me mettre au courant de la Femme!
Nous lui dirons d'abord, de mon air le moins froid:
"La somme des angles d'un triangle, chère âme,
      Est égale à deux droits."

Et si ce cri lui part: "Dieu de Dieu! que je t'aime!"
"Dieu reconnaîtra les siens." Ou piquée au vif:
"Mes claviers ont du cœur, tu seras mon seul thème."
      Moi: "Tout est relatif."
De tous ses yeux, alors! se sentant trop banale:
"Ah! tu ne m'aimes pas; tant d'autres sont jaloux!"
Et moi, d'un œil qui vers l'Inconscient s'emballe:
      "Merci, pas mal; et vous?"

"Jouons au plus fidèle!" "A quoi bon, ô Nature!"
"Autant à qui perd gagne!" Alors, autre couplet:
"Ah! tu te lasseras le premier, j'en suis sûre . . . "
      "Après vous, s'il vous plaît."

Enfin, si, par un soir, elle meurt dans mes livres,
Douce; feignant de n'en pas croire encor mes yeux,
J'aurai un: "Ah ça, mais, nous avions De Quoi vivre!
      C'était donc sérieux?"

# ANOTHER COMPLAINT
# OF LORD PIERROT

She who is to put me in touch with Woman!
Let's say to her first, with the mildest of stares,
"The sum of a triangle's angles, dear soul,
      Is equal to two squares."

And if she should cry out, "Oh God! I love you so!"
"God will look after His own." Or, pierced to the bone:
"My heartstrings have feelings; for you alone I live!"
      I: "Everything is relative."

Then, with blazing eyes! renouncing banality:
"Ah, you don't really love me; and so many envy you."
Then, with my eyes bolting toward the Unconscious:
      "Thanks, not so bad, and you?"

"Let's play Fidelity!" "O Nature, what's the use?"
"But what can you lose, after all!" And then, *reprise*:
"Oh! you'll get tired of it first, I'm sure . . ."
      "After you, if you please."

And at last, if, some evening, she dies among my books,
Pretending not to believe my eyes, invoke,
Sweetly: "Oh dear! but we had Something to Live For!
      Was it, then—no joke?"

# COMPLAINTE
## SUR CERTAINS ENNUIS

Un couchant des Cosmogonies!
Ah! que la Vie est quotidienne . . .
Et, du plus vrai qu'on se souvienne,
Comme on fut piètre et sans génie . . .

On voudrait s'avouer des choses,
Dont on s'étonnerait en route,
Qui feraient, une fois pour toutes!
Qu'on s'entendrait à travers poses.

On voudrait saigner le Silence,
Secouer l'exil des causeries;
Et non! ces dames sont aigries
Par des questions de préséance.

Elles boudent là, l'air capable.
Et, sous le ciel, plus d'un s'explique,
Par quel gâchis suresthétiques
Ces êtres-là sont adorables.

Justement, une nous appelle,
Pour l'aider à chercher sa bague,
Perdue (où dans ce terrain vague?)
Un souvenir D'AMOUR, dit-elle!

Ces êtres-là sont adorables!

# COMPLAINT
# ABOUT CERTAIN ANNOYANCES

A sunset of Cosmogonies!
Ah! this Life is so everyday . . .
And, for the best of memories,
The paltry talents we display . . .

What about those confidences,
Those mutual revelations,
Which were to show us, once and for all,
The way through our self-defences?

We wanted to bleed the Silence,
Shake off the exile of conversation;
But no! the ladies have grown sour
Evaluating rank and station.

They pout over there with a capable air.
And, under the sky, more than one of us wonders
By just what superaesthetic blunders
These creatures are adorable.

Here's one of them now, requesting me
To help look for her ring,
Lost (but where in this vacant lot?),
A souvenir of LOVE, says she.

Who said they aren't adorable!

## COMPLAINTE
## DU PAUVRE CORPS HUMAIN

L'homme et sa compagne sont serfs
De corps, tourbillonnants cloaques
Aux mailles de harpes de nerfs
Serves de tout et que détraque
Un fier répertoire d'attaques.

      Voyez l'homme, voyez!
      Si ça n'fait pas pitié!

Propre et correct en ses ressorts,
S'assaisonnant de modes vaines,
Il s'admire, ce brave corps,
Et s'endimanche pour sa peine,
Quand il a bien sué la semaine.

      Et sa compagne! allons,
      Ma bell', nous nous valons.

Faudrait le voir, touchant et nu
Dans un décor d'oiseaux, de roses;
Ses tics réflexes d'ingénu,
Ses plis pris de mondaines poses;
Bref, sur beau fond vert, sa chlorose.

      Voyez l'homme, voyez!
      Si ça n'fait pas pitié!

Les Vertus et les Voluptés
Détraquent d'un rien sa machine,
Il ne vit que pour disputer
Ce domaine à rentes divines
Aux lois de mort qui le taquinent.

# COMPLAINT
# CONCERNING THE POOR HUMAN BODY

Man and his wife: to the body
Slaves, whirlpooling sewers
Webbed with harp-string nerves,
Serfs to all and jumping their tracks
Under miscellaneous attacks.

> That's man, all right!
> Sorry sight!

Proper and sure in its reactions,
Sparked with the latest chic,
This body's proud of its attractions,
Eager to dress up Sunday-sleek
When it has sweated out the week.

> And his wife! between us two,
> Girl, either will do.

You should see it, touching and nude,
In a decor of birds and roses;
Ingenuous reflexes, its tics,
Gestures copied from worldly poses;
On a green background, jaundice-hued.

> That's man, all right!
> Sorry sight!

Virtues and voluptuous Vice
Are poisonous to his machine,
Living only for the fight
Between its divinely established domain
And the death-clause fingering its brain.

Et sa compagne! allons,
Ma bell', nous nous valons.

Il se soutient de mets pleins d'art,
Se drogue, se tond, se parfume,
Se truffe tant, qu'il meurt trop tard;
Et la cuisine se résume
En mille infections posthumes.

Oh! ce couple, voyez!
Non, ça fait trop pitié.

Mais ce microbe subversif
Ne compte pas pour la Substance,
Dont les déluges corrosifs
Renoient vite pour l'Innocence
Ces fols germes de conscience.
Nature est sans pitié
Pour son petit dernier.

And his wife! between us two,
Girl, either will do.

Supported by artistic corrections,
Drugs, hairdressers, perfumes,
It stuffs itself for a belated defection;
And then the cooking resumes
In a thousand posthumous infections.

Oh! Look at this pair!
No. A pitiful affair.

But that brief subversive microbe
Doesn't matter to the Whole
Whose corrosive inundations
Drown quickly again for Innocence
Those crazy sprouts of cerebration.

Nature has only scorn
For her last-born.

## COMPLAINTE
## DU ROI DE THULÉ

Il était un roi de Thulé,
          Immaculé,
Qui, loin des jupes et des choses,
Pleurait sur la métempsycose
          Des lys en roses,
          Et quel palais!


Ses fleurs dormant, il s'en allait,
          Traînant des clés,
Broder aux seuls yeux des étoiles,
Sur une tour, un certain Voile,
          De vive toile,
          Aux nuits de lait!


Quand le voile fut bien ourlé,
          Loin de Thulé,
Il rama fort sur les mers grises,
Vers le soleil qui s'agonise,
          Féerique Église!
          Il ululait:


"Soleil-crevant, encore un jour,
Vous avez tendu votre phare
Aux holocaustes vivipares,
Du culte qu'ils nomment l'Amour.


"Et comme, devant la nuit fauve,
Vous vous sentez défaillir,
D'un dernier flot d'un sang martyr
Vous lavez le seuil de l'Alcôve!

# COMPLAINT
# OF THE KING OF THULE

There once was a king of Thule
    Devoted to purity.
To stay far from skirts he proposes,
And weeps for the metempsycosis
    Of lilies to roses,
    In his palace close to the sea.

When his flowers were all asleep,
    He left, laden with keys,
To weave where only the stars could see,
High on a tower, a certain Veil,
    Embroidered with night's
    White light.

When he finished its embroidery,
    Far from Thule,
Hard he rowed across the gray seas
Toward the sun's final agonies,
    Magical Grail!
    He wailed:

"Dying Sun, once more till dusk
Your light has reached us from above
Toward the viviparous holocausts
Of the cult that they call love.

And, as before the beasts of night
You feel yourself losing your hold,
With a last flood of martyred blood
You wash the Alcove's threshold!

"Soleil! Soleil! moi je descends
Vers vos navrants palais polaires,
Dorloter dans ce Saint-Suaire
      Votre cœur bien en sang,
      En le berçant!"


Il dit, et, le Voile étendu,
      Tout éperdu,
Vers les coraux et les naufrages,
Le roi raillé des doux corsages,
      Beau comme un Mage
      Est descendu!


Braves amants! aux nuits de lait,
      Tournez vos clés!
Une ombre, d'amour pur transie,
Viendrait vous gémir cetter scie:
"Il était un roi de Thulé
      Immaculé . . . "

Sun! O Sun! I come down
Toward your harrowing polar citadels,
To shelter in this Sacred Shroud
        Your bleeding heart,
        And rock it well!"

He said, with the Veil extended
        Fervently,
Toward the corals and sunken wrecks,
The king mocked by gentle breasts,
        Like a Mage, and beautiful,
        Descended!

O lovers! when white nights prey,
        Turn the key!
Frozen by purest love, a shade
Will come to seek you and complain:
"There was a king of Thule
        Devoted to purity . . . "

## COMPLAINTE
## DE L'OUBLI DES MORTS

Mesdames et Messieurs,
Vous dont la mère est morte.
C'est le bon fossoyeux
Qui gratte à votre porte.

Les morts
C'est sous terre;
Ça n'en sort
Guère.

Vous fumez dans vos bocks,
Vous soldez quelque idylle,
Là-bas chante le coq,
Pauvres morts hors des villes!

Grand-papa se penchait,
Là, le doigt sur la tempe,
Sœur faisait du crochet,
Mère montait la lampe.

Les morts
C'est discret,
Ça dort
Trop au frais.

Vous avez bien dîné,
Comment va cette affaire?
Ah! les petite mort-nés
Ne se dorlotent guère!

Notez, d'un trait égal,
Au livre de la caisse,

# COMPLAINT
# ABOUT FORGETTING THE DEAD

Ladies and Gentlemen,
You whose mother is no more,
Listen! the good gravedigger's
Knocking at your door.

The dead
Underground
Hardly ever
Get around.

You blow into your beer,
Wrap up your dreams and pay;
Down there the chanticleer,
The poor dead, out of the way!

Grandpapa would sway,
Heavy head on hand,
Sister did crochet,
Mother lit the lamp.

The dead—
So discreet,
Too much air
Where they sleep.

Now you've had your dinner;
How was business today?
Ah! the stillborn babies
Scarcely ever play.

Tell that steady hand to place
Neatly in your budget,

Entre deux frais de bal:
Entretien tombe et messe.

    C'est gai,
  Cette vie;
    Hein, ma mie,
  O gué?

Mesdames et Messieurs,
Vous dont la sœur est morte,
Ouvrez au fossoyeux
Qui claque à votre porte;

Si vous n'avez pitié,
Il viendra (sans rancune)
Vous tirer par les pieds,
Une nuit de grand'lune!

    Importun
  Vent qui rage!
  Les défunts?
  Ça voyage.

Your wardrobe won't begrudge it:
Upkeep on the graves.

Life's gay,
Take a whirl;
Eh! girl,
OK?

Ladies and Gentlemen,
You whose sister is no more,
A welcome for the gravedigger
Banging on your door!
If you can't be polite,
He'll come (but not for spite)
And drag you by your feet
Into some moonlit night!

Wild winds unravel
Overhead;
And the dead?
Travel.

# COMPLAINTE
# DU PAUVRE JEUNE HOMME

Sur l'air populaire:<br>
"Quand le bonhomm' revient du bois."

Quand ce jeune homm' rentra chez lui,
Quand ce jeune homm' rentra chez lui,
Il prit à deux mains son vieux crâne,
Qui de science était un puits!
     Crâne,
      Riche crâne,
Entends-tu la Folie qui plane?
Et qui demande le cordon,
Digue dondaine, digue dondaine,
Et qui demande le cordon,
Digue dondaine, digue dondon?

Quand ce jeune homm' rentra chez lui,
Quand ce jeune homm' rentra chez lui,
Il entendit de tristes gammes,
Qu'un piano pleurait dans la nuit!
     Gammes
      Vieilles gammes,
Ensemble, enfants, nous vous cherchâmes;
Son mari m'a fermé sa maison,
Digue dondaine, digue dondaine,
Son mari m'a fermé sa maison,
Digue dondaine, digue dondon!

Quand ce jeune homm' rentra chez lui,
Quand ce jeune homm' rentra chez lui,
Il mit le nez dans sa belle âme,
Où fermentaient des tas d'ennuis!
     Ame,

# COMPLAINT
# CONCERNING A POOR YOUNG MAN

To the popular tune:
"Quand le bonhomm' revient du bois."

When the young man returned to his home,
When the young man returned to his home,
He took in both hands his old skull,
With science almost overgrown!
     Skull,
       Rich skull!
Would you that Madness annul?
Listen! It wants to come in,
Ding dong ding-a-ling,
Listen! It wants to come in,
Ding-a-ling ding dong!

When the young man returned to his home,
When the young man returned to his home,
He heard some melancholy tunes
In the night, an old piano's groans!
     Tunes,
       Old tunes,
Children, we were looking for you!
Her husband won't let me come in,
Ding dong ding-a-ling,
Her husband won't let me come in,
Ding-a-ling ding dong!

When the young man to his home returned,
When the young man to his home returned,
He stuck his nose in his beautiful soul
Where all kinds of troubles churned!
     Soul,

Ma belle âme,
Leur huile est trop sal' pour ta flamme!
Puis, nuit partout! lors, à quoi bon?
Digue dondaine, digue dondaine,
Puis, nuit partout! lors, à quoi bon?
Digue dondaine, digue dondon!

Quand ce jeune homm' rentra chez lui,
Quand ce jeune homm' rentra chez lui,
Il vit que sa charmante femme,
Avait déménagé sans lui!
    Dame,
     Notre-Dame,
Je n'aurai pas un mot de blâme!
Mais t'aurais pu laisser l'charbon,[1]
Digue dondaine, digue dondaine,
Mais t'aurais pu laisser l'charbon,
Digue dondaine, digue dondon.
Lors, ce jeune homme aux tels ennuis,
Lors, ce jeune homme aux tels ennuis,
Alla décrocher une lame,
Qu'on lui avait fait cadeau avec l'étui!
    Lame
     Fine lame,
Soyez plus droite que la femme!
Et vous, mon Dieu, pardon! pardon!
Digue dondaine, digue dondaine,
Et vous, mon Dieu, pardon! pardon!
Digue dondaine, digue dondon!

Quand les croq'morts vinrent chez lui,
Quand les croq'morts vinrent chez lui;

---

1    Pour s'asphyxier

Beautiful soul,
On their crude oil your flame won't burn!
So what's the use? Oh, night alone!
Ding dong ding-a-ling,
So what's the use? Oh, night alone!
Ding-a-ling ding dong.

When the young man returned to his home,
When the young man returned to his home,
He saw that his faithful love
Had packed up and left him alone!
Love,
God above!
No words will do well enough!
But the coal! You could have left me some,[1]
Ding dong ding-a-ling,
But the coal! You could have left me some,
Ding-a-ling ding dong.

Then the young man so much betrayed,
Then the young man so much betrayed,
Went to take down his knife,
A present, case and blade!
Knife,
Sharp knife,
Be you more true than my wife!
And you, O God, I beg your pardon!
Ding dong ding-a-ling,
And you, O God, I beg your pardon!
Ding-a-ling ding dong!
When the croakers came to his door,
When the croakers came to his door;

---

1    To kill himself with

Ils virent qu' c'était un' belle âme,
Comme on n'en fait plus aujourd'hui.
       Ame,
         Dors, belle âme!
Quand on est mort, c'est pour de bon,
Digue dondaine, digue dondaine,
Quand on est mort, c'est pour de bon,
Digue dondaine, digue dondon!

They saw that it was a beautiful soul,
The kind that nobody makes any more.
  Soul,
   Sleep, beautiful soul!
When you're dead it's for so long,
Ding dong ding-a-ling,
When you're dead it's for so long,
Ding-a-ling ding dong!

# COMPLAINTE
## DE L'ÉPOUX OUTRAGÉ

Sur l'air populaire:
"Qu'allais-tu faire à la fontaine?"

—Qu'alliez-vous faire à la Mad'leine,
     Corbleu, ma moitié,
Qu'alliez-vous faire à la Mad'leine?

—J'allais prier pour qu'un fils nous vienne,
     Mon Dieu, mon ami;
J'allais prier pour qu'un fils nous vienne.

—Vous vous teniez dans un coin, debout,
     Corbleu, ma moitié!
Vous vous teniez dans un coin, debout.

—Pas d'chaise économis' trois sous,
     Mon Dieu, mon ami;
Pas d'chaise économis' trois sous.

—D'un officier, j'ai vu la tournure,
     Corbleu, ma moitié!
D'un officier, j'ai vu la tournure.

—C'était le Christ grandeur nature,
     Mon Dieu, mon ami;
C'était le Christ grandeur nature.

—Les Christs n'ont pas la croix d'honneur,
     Corbleu, ma moitié!
Les Christs n'ont pas la croix d'honneur.

# COMPLAINT
# OF THE OUTRAGED HUSBAND

On the popular tune:
"Qu'allais-tu faire a la fontaine?"

—Why did you go to the church today,
     By God! spouse,
Why did you go to the church today?

—That we'd have a son I went to pray,
     Really, my dear;
That we'd have a son I went to pray.

—You were standing in a corner there,
     By God! spouse,
You were standing in a corner there.

—It costs three cents to have a chair,
     Really, my dear;
It costs three cents to have a chair.

—I saw an officer, tall and lean,
     By God! spouse,
I saw an officer, tall and lean.

—It was the life-size Christ you mean,
     Really, my dear;
It was the life-size Christ you mean.

—Christs don't wear the Silver Star,
     By God, spouse!
Christs don't wear the Silver Star!

—C'était la plaie du Calvaire, au cœur,
    Mon Dieu, mon ami;
C'était la plaie du Calvaire, au cœur.


—Les Christs n'ont qu'au flanc seul la plaie,
    Corbleu, ma moitié!
Les Christs n'ont qu'au flanc seul la plaie!


—C'était une goutte envolée,
    Mon Dieu, mon ami;
C'était une goutte envolée.


—Aux Crucifix on n'parl' jamais,
    Corbleu, ma moitié!
Aux Crucifix on n'parl' jamais.


—C'était du trop d'amour qu' j'avais,
    Mon Dieu, mon ami,
C'était du trop d'amour qu' j'avais!


—Et moi j'te brûl'rai la cervelle,
    Corbleu, ma moitié,
Et moi, j'te brûl'rai la cervelle!


—Lui, il aura mon âme immortelle,
    Mon Dieu, mon ami,
Lui, il aura mon âme immortelle!

—Of Calvary it was a scar,
      Really, my dear;
Of Calvary it was a scar.

—The wound of Christ is in His side,
      By God, spouse!
The wound of Christ is in His side!

—On His heart a drop of blood had dried,
      Really, my dear;
On His heart a drop of blood had dried.

—Who ever talks to the Crucifix,
      By God, spouse!
Who ever talks to the Crucifix?

—Too much love made me prolix,
      Really, my dear,
Too much love made me prolix!

—Through your head I'll drill a hole,
      By God! spouse,
Through your head I'll drill a hole!

—Then He'll have my immortal soul,
      Really, my dear,
He'll have my immortal soul!

# COMPLAINTE DES DÉBATS
# MÉLANCOLIQUES ET LITTÉRAIRES

On peut encore aimer, mais confier toute son âme
est un bonheur qu'on ne retrouvera plus.
*Corinne ou l'Italie*

Le long d'un ciel crépusculaire,
Une cloche angéluse en paix
L'air exilescent et marâtre
Qui ne pardonnera jamais.

Paissant des débris de vaisselle,
Là-bas, au talus des remparts,
Se profile une haridelle
Convalescente; il se fait tard.

Qui m'aima jamais? Je m'entête
Sur ce refrain bien impuissant,
Sans songer que je suis bien bête
De me faire du mauvais sang.

Je possède un propre physique,
Un cœur d'enfant bien élevé,
Et pour un cerveau magnifique
Le mien n'est pas mal, vous savez.

Eh bien, ayant pleuré l'Histoire,
J'ai voulu vivre un brin heureux;
C'était trop demander, faut croire;
J'avais l'air de parler hébreux.

Ah! tiens, mon cœur, de grâce, laisse!
Lorsque j'y songe, en vérité,
J'en ai des sueurs de faiblesse,
A choir dans la malpropreté.

# COMPLAINT CONCERNING
# MELANCHOLY AND LITERARY DEBATES

> Love is still possible; but to commit all one's soul
> is a happiness not to be found again.
>
> *Corinne; or, Italy*

Along a twilightish sky,
Angelusing bells fling peace
At an exilescent stepmotherly air;
No forgiveness there.

Feeding on broken crockery,
Down there on the hill by the fortress gate
In profile appears a convalescent
Nag; it's getting late.

Who ever loved me? I begin
Again that impotent refrain,
Not seeing how foolish I remain
To let it get under my skin.

I have a pleasantly fitted physique,
The heart of a well brought up child,
And if it's magnificent minds you seek,
You could do worse than mine.

Well, having wept over History,
I wanted to take out a lease
On a bit of happiness; no deal.
I seemed to be talking Chinese.

Ah! my heart, that's enough! Please!
Whenever I can't forget, you know,
My weaknesses break out in a sweat
Until, unclean, I let myself go.

Le cœur me piaffe de génie
Éperdument pourtant, mon Dieu!
Et si quelqu'une veut ma vie,
Moi je ne demande pas mieux!

Eh va, pauvre âme véhémente!
Plonge, être, en leurs Jourdains blasés,
Deux frictions de vie courante
T'auront vite exorcisé.

Hélas, qui peut m'en répondre!
Tenez, peut-être savez-vous
Ce que c'est qu'une âme hypocondre?
J'en suis une dans les prix doux.

O Hélène, j'erre en ma chambre;
Et tandis que tu prends le thé,
Là-bas dans l'or d'un fier septembre,
Je frissonne de tous mes membres,
En m'inquiétant de ta santé.

Tandis que, d'un autre côté . . .

*Berlin*

Under my genius my heart curvets,
But, I tell you, just desperately!
If some young lady wants my life,
That's quite all right with me!

Oh go on, poor being, vehement soul!
Into their blasé Jordans, dive;
Just twice massaged with running life
And you'll be exorcized.

Who can answer me, alas?
You there, perhaps you know
What to do with a hypochondriac
Soul? Mine's really first-class.

O Helen, I roam my room;
And while you're far away drinking tea,
In some September day's proud wealth,
My whole body shivers feverishly,
I'm so worried about your health.

True, from another point of view . . .

*Berlin*

# COMPLAINTE
# D'UNE CONVALESCENCE EN MAI

> Nous n'avons su toutes ces choses qu'après sa mort.
>
> *Vie de Pascal,* par M^me Périer

Convalescent au lit, ancré de courbatures,
Je me plains aux dessins bleus de ma couverture,

Las de reconstituer dans l'art du jour baissant
Cette dame d'en face auscultant les passants.

Si la Mort, de son van, avait choisi mon être,
En serait-elle moins, ce soir, à sa fenêtre? . . .

Oh! mort, tout mort! au plus jamais, au vrai néant
Des nuits où piaule en longs regrets le chant-huant!

Et voilà que mon Ame est tout hallucinée!
Mais s'abat, sans avoir fixé sa destinée.

Ah! que de soirs de mai pareils à celui-ci;
Que la vie est égale; et le cœur endurci!

Je me sens fou d'un tas de petites misères.
Mais maintenant, je sais ce qu'il me reste à faire.

Qui m'a jamais rêvé? Je voudrais le savoir!
Elle vous sourient avec âme, et puis bonsoir,

Ni vu ni connu. Et les voilà qui rebrodent
Le canevas ingrat de leur âme à la mode;

Fraîches à tous, et puis reprenant leur air sec
Pour les christs déclassés et autre gens suspects.

# COMPLAINT
# ABOUT A CONVALESCENCE IN MAY

> We knew all those things only after his death.
> *Life of Pascal,* by Mme Périer

In bed, convalescing, anchored to my pain,
To the blue designs on my quilt I complain,

Tired of reconstructing, with the art of the dying day,
That lady across the street auscultating passers-by.

If winnowing Death had picked up my being,
Would she be, any less, at her window this evening? . . .

Oh! dead, utterly dead! Forever, in the Abyss
Of nights where an owl whimpers its long regrets.

And there's my Soul, all for hallucination,
But falls without selecting a destination.

Ah, how many more May evenings like this one,
With the heart grown hard, and life no fun.

I've been driven mad by a bunch of trivialities
But at least I know what's left to do about me.

Whose dream was I ever? I'd like to know!
They smile at you soulfully, and go;

Out of sight, out of mind. On tough canvases, after a while,
They reinvent their souls in the latest style

New for all comers, and then they dryly inspect
Down-at-heel Christs, and others they suspect.

Et pourtant, le béni grand bol de lait de ferme
Que me serait un baiser sur sa bouche ferme!

Je ne veux accuser personne, bien qu'on eût
Pu, ce me semble, mon bon cœur étant connu . . .

N'est-ce pas; nous savons ce qu'il nous reste à faire,
O Cœur d'Or pétri d'aromates littéraires,

Et toi, cerveau confit dans l'alcool de l'Orgueil!
Et qu'il faut procéder d'abord par demi-deuils . . .

Primo: mes grandes angoisses métaphysiques
Sont passées à l'état de chagrins domestiques;

Deux ou trois spleens locaux.—Ah, pitié, voyager
Du moins, pendant un an ou deux à l'étranger . . .

Plonger mon front dans l'eau des mers, aux matinées
Torrides, m'en aller à petites journées,

Compter les clochers, puis m'asseoir, ayant très chaud,
Aveuglé des maisons peintes au lait de chaux—

Dans les Indes du Rêve aux pacifiques Ganges,
Que j'en ai des comptoirs, des hamacs de rechange!

—Voici l'œuf à la coque et la lampe du soir.
Convalescence bien folle, comme on peut voir.

*Coblentz*

And yet, to kiss those firm lips, fresh and warm
Like a blessed bowl of milk straight from a farm!

I'm not accusing anyone, but they could
Have, it seems to me; my heart's well known to be good . . .

Don't you think? We know where we'll have to resume,
O Heart of Gold embalmed in literary perfume,

And you, brain put up in alcoholic Conceit!
First, in half-mourning, we'll proceed . . .

Yes. My anguished metaphysical cerebrations
Have faded to domestic complications,

Two or three local complaints. Oh please!
How about going abroad for a year or two at least . . .

On torrid mornings, bathe my head in the sea,
Make pleasant little excursions, take my time,

Count towers, then sit down, too hot, half-blind
From the houses painted white with lime—

In Indias of Dream where peaceful Ganges curve,
I've plenty of trading-posts and hammocks in reserve!

—Here's my soft-boiled egg, and the evening light.
A crazy convalescence, you're quite right.

*Coblentz*

from

# *L'IMITATION DE NOTRE-DAME LA LUNE*

# LITANIES
# DES PREMIERS QUARTIERS DE LA LUNE

Lune bénie
Des insomnies,

Blanc médaillon
Des Endymions,

Astre fossile
Que tout exile,

Jaloux tombeau
De Salammbô,

Embarcadère
Des grands Mystères,

Madone et miss
Diane-Artémis,

Sainte Vigie
De nos orgies,

Jettatura
Des baccarats,

Dame très lasse
De nos terrasses,

Philtre attisant
Les vers-luisants,

# LITANIES
# FOR THE FIRST QUARTERS OF THE MOON

Blessed light
Of sleepless nights,

Endymion's
White medalion,

Fossil star,
Exiled afar,

Jealous tomb
Of Salammbo,

Station
For mystification,

Madonna and Miss,
Diana-Artemis,

Holy Watch
Of our debauch,

Croupier
At every play,

Lady so wan
Pacing our lawn,

Philter to energize
Fireflies,

Rosace et dôme
Des derniers psaumes,

Bel oeil-de-chat
De nos rachats,

Sois l'Ambulance
De nos croyances!

Sois l'édredon
Du Grand-Pardon!

Rose window and dome
Of the final psalms,

Cat's eye, ornament
Of our atonement,

Be the Relief
For our belief,

Be a Quilt
For all our guilt!

# PIERROTS

I.

C'est, sur un cou qui, raide, émerge
D'une fraise empesée idem,
Une face imberbe au cold-cream,
Un air d'hydrocéphale asperge.

Les yeux sont noyés de l'opium
De l'indulgence universelle,
La bouche clownesque ensorcele
Comme un singulier géranium.

Bouche qui va du trou sans bonde
Glacialement désopilé,
Au transcendental en-ailé
Du souris vain de la Joconde.

Campant leur cône enfariné
Sur le noir serre-tête en soie,
Ils font rire leur patte d'oie
Et froncent en trèfle leur nez.

Ils ont comme chaton de bague
Le scarabée égyptien,
A leur boutonnière fait bien
Le pissenlit des terrains vagues.

Ils vont, se sustentant d'azur,
Et parfois aussi de légumes,
De riz plus blanc que leur costume,
De mandarines et d'œufs durs.

# PIERROTS

### I.

It's, on a stiff neck emerging thus
From similarly starchèd lace,
A callow under cold-cream face
Like hydrocephalic asparagus.

The eyes are drowned in the opium
Of universal clemency,
The clown-like mouth bewitches
Like a peculiar geranium.

A mouth which goes from an unplugged hole
Of refrigerated levity,
To that winged transcendental aisle
And vain, the Gioconda's smile.

Flour-sprinkled, a cone reposes
On their headband of black silk,
They make their crow's-feet giggle,
Indenting to trefoils their noses.

In their finger rings are not
Jewels but Egyptian scarabs,
For their buttonholes they adopt
Dandelions from vacant lots.

Pierrots feed on the absolute,
And sometimes on vegetables too,
On rice whiter than their costume,
On hard-boiled eggs and fruit.

Ils sont de la secte du Blême,
Ils n'ont rien à voir avec Dieu,
Et sifflent: "Tout est pour le mieux
Dans la meilleur' des mi-carême!"

To the Pallid Sect they belong
"God's not for us!" they protest;
Whistling, "All is for the best
When the Carnaval comes along!"

## II.

Le cœur blanc tatoué
De sentences lunaires,
Ils ont: "Faut mourir, frères!"
Pour mot-d'ordre-Évohé.

Quand trépasse une vierge,
Ils suivent son convoi,
Tenant leur cou tout droit
Comme on porte un beau cierge.

Rôle très fatigant,
D'autant qu'ils n'ont personne
Chez eux, qui les frictionne
D'un conjugal onguent.

Ces dandys de la Lune
S'imposent, en effet,
De chanter "S'il vous plaît?"
De la blonde à la brune.

Car c'est des gens blasés;
Et s'ils vous semblent dupes,
Ça et là, de la Jupe,
Lange à cicatriser,

Croyez qu'ils font la bête
Afin d'avoir des seins,
Pis-aller des coussins
A leurs savantes têtes.

II

Their white hearts tattooed
With maxims of lunar design,
They have "We'll die, my brothers!"
For Bacchic countersign.

Whenever a virgin dies
They follow the funeral,
Holding their necks up high
Like ceremonial candles.

A very tiring appointment
Because, you see, there's no one
At home for their massage
With matrimonial ointment.

These dandies of the Moon
Believe themselves assigned
From blonde to brunette
To sing "If you don't mind?"

For them it's a worn-out game,
And if they seem to be hurt
Now and then by the Skirt
Which might have bandaged pain,

Remember they play the fool
In order to have breasts,
Better than no pillows
Where their wise heads rest.

Écarquillant le cou
Et feignant de comprendre
De travers, la voix tendre,
Mais les yeux si filous !

—D'ailleurs, de mœurs très fines,
Et toujours fort corrects,
(École des cromlechs
Et des tuyaux d'usines).

Stretching out their necks
And pretending to understand
All wrong, their voices bland,
But pickpocket eyes!

—Moreover, they act like gentlemen,
Observant of the Social Rule
(According to the Dolmen
And Factory Smokestack School.)

III

Comme ils vont molester, la nuit,
Au profond des parcs, les statues,
Mais n'offrant qu'aux moins dévêtues
Leurs bras et tout ce qui s'ensuit,

En tête à tête avec la femme
Ils ont toujours l'air d'être un tiers,
Confondent demain avec hier,
Et demandent Rien avec âme!

Jurent "je t'aime!" l'air là-bas,
D'une voix sans timbre, en extase,
Et concluent aux plus folles phrases
Par des: "Mon Dieu, n'insistons pas?"

Jusqu'à ce qu'ivre, Elle s'oublie,
Prise d'on ne sait quel besoin
De lune? dans leurs bras, fort loin
Des convenances établies.

III

When they, in the dark, go off to molest
The statues deep in the park,
And offer (to the least undressed)
Their arms and all the rest;

When they with Woman converse apart
They always seem to make a third,
Confuse tomorrow with yesterday,
And ask for Nothing with all their hearts!

Swearing "I love you," their style second-rate,
With toneless voices, in ecstacy,
And concluding the wildest rhapsodies
With "Good Lord! Perhaps I exaggerate?"

Until, drunk out of her mind, She
Is—who knows why?—disposed to crave
The moon? and in their arms to flee
The way young ladies should behave.

IV

Maquillés d'abandon, les manches
En saule, ils leur font des serments,
Pour être vrais trop véhéments!
Puis tumultuent en gigues blanches.

Beuglant, Ange! tu m'as compris
A la vie, à la mort!—et songent:
Ah! passer là-dessus l'éponge! . . .
Et ce n'est pas chez eux parti pris,

Hélas! mais l'idée de la femme
Se prenant au sérieux encor
Dans ce siècle, voilà, les tord
D'un rire aux déchirantes gammes!

Ne leur jetez pas la pierre, ô
Vous qu'affecte une jarretière!
Allez, ne jetez pas la pierre
Aux blancs parias, aux pure Pierrots!

IV

Made up with negligence, their sleeves
Willowy, they offer vows
Too vehement to be believed!
Then in wild white jigs convulse,

Bellowing, "Angel! You understand me,
Forever and ever!" but, sotto voce:
"Ah! to rub out all this! . . ."
And from them it's not just prejudice,

Alas, but the thought of these females
Taking themselves still seriously
In this century, you see, explodes
Their laughter in heart-rending scales!

Don't throw stones at them, O
You, upset by fancy garters!
I tell you don't throw stones
At the white pariah, the pure Pierrot.

V.

Blancs enfants de choeur de la Lune,
Et lunologues éminents,
Leur Église ouvre à tout venant,
Claire, d'ailleurs, comme pas une,

Ils disent, d'un oeil faisandé,
Les manches très sacerdotales,
Que ce bas monde de scandale
N'est qu'un des mille coups de dé

Du jeu que l'Idée et l'Amour,
Afin sans doute de connaître
Aussi leur propre raison d'être
Ont jugé bon de mettre au jour.

Que nul d'ailleurs ne vaut le nôtre,
Qu'il faut pas le traiter d'hôtel
Garni vers un plus immortel,
Car nous sommes faits l'un pour l'autre;

Qu'enfin, et rien de moins subtil,
Ces gratuites antinomies
Au fond ne nous regardant mie,
L'art de tout est l'Ainsi soit-il;

Et que, chers frères, le beau rôle
Est de vivre de but en blanc
Et, dût-on se battre les flancs,
De hausser à tout les épaules.

## V.

White choirboys of the Moon
And eminent lunologists,
Their Church open to anyone,
And clear, as no other that exists;

They say, with well-seasoned eyes,
Their sleeves ecclesiastically curled,
That all this low scandalous world
Is just one of a thousand throws of the dice

In the game that the Idea and Love
In order, no doubt, to discover
Their own existence justified,
Have thought it best to uncover.

That none, moreover, is worth our own—
Don't treat it like a furnished room
On route to some more immortal home,
Since we were made for each other;

And, after all, it's obvious
That their quite gratuitous argument
Has nothing, in fact, to do with us—
Let's say "Amen," not make a fuss.

And, dear brothers, the best of tricks
Is to live full speed ahead! growing older;
If you have to kick against the pricks,
At everything shrug your shoulder.

# PIERROTS

*(Scène courte, mais typique.)*

Il me faut, vos yeux! Dès que je perds leur étoile,
Le mal des calmes plats s'engouffre dans ma voile,
Le frisson du Vae soli gargouille en mes moelles . . .

Vous auriez dû me voir après cette querelle!
J'errais dans l'agitation la plus cruelle,
Criant aux murs: Mon Dieu! mon Dieu! Que dira-t-elle?

Mais aussi, vrai, vous me blessâtes aux antennes
De l'âme, avec les mensonges de votre traîne,
Et votre tas de complications mondaines.

Je voyais que vos yeux me lançaient sur des pistes,
Je songeais: Oui, divins, ces yeux! mais rien n'existe
Derrière! Son âme est affaire d'oculiste.

Moi, je suis laminé d'esthétiques loyales!
Je hais les trémolos, les phrases nationales;
Bref, le violet gros deuil est ma couleur locale.

Je ne suis point "ce gaillard-là" ni Le Superbe!
Mais mon âme, qu'un cri un peu cru exacerbe,
Est au fond distinguée et franche comme une herbe.

J'ai des nerfs encor sensibles au son des cloches,
Et je vais en plein air sans peur et sans reproche,
Sans jamais me sourire en un miroir de poche.

C'est vrai, j'ai bien roulé! J'ai râlé dans des gîtes
Peu vous; mais, n'en ai-je pas plus de mérite
A en avoir sauvé la foi en vos yeux? dites . . .

# PIERROTS

(A short but typical scene)

But I need your eyes! As soon as I lose their rays
The sickness of dead calms engulfs my sails,
The shiver of Vae soli! gurgles in my veins . . .

You should have seen me after that argument!
I wandered about in the cruellest kind of torment,
Crying to the walls: My God! My God! Will she relent?

But just the same you wounded the antennae
Of my soul with all your trailing lies,
And all you think your social life requires.

I saw your eyes were daring me to dare;
I thought: Oh yes, divine! those eyes, but nothing's there
Behind them. Her soul's an oculist's affair.

Aesthetics laminate me, and they're true!
I hate the tremolo, the nationalistic hullabaloo;
In short, deep purple mourning's my native hue.

No one says "stout fellow!" or "Superb!"
But my soul, which even a raspy cry can disturb,
Is candid and distinguished, like an herb.

My nerves can still respond to ringing bells I hear,
I go about in the open air, guileless and without fear,
And never, passing mirrors, smile and peer.

It's true, I've knocked around! I've spent my time in ways
Not at all yours; but don't I deserve the more praise
For never losing faith in your eyes? Say . . .

—Allons, faisons la paix. Venez, que je vous berce,
Enfant. Eh bien?
—C'est que, votre pardon me verse
Un mélange (confus) d'impressions . . . diverses . . .
*(Exit.)*

—Oh, let's make up! Come sit on my lap,
Dear child. What now?
—I just don't know how to take
Being forgiven  . . . for what? And so late . . .
*(Exit.)*

# LOCUTIONS DES PIERROTS

I.

Les mares de vos yeux aux joncs de cils,
O vaillante oisive femme,
Quand donc me renverront-ils
La Lune-levante de ma belle âme?

Voilà tantôt une heure qu'en langueur
Mon cœur si simple s'abreuve
De vos vilaines rigueurs,
Avec le regard bon d'un terre-neuve.

Ah! madame, ce n'est vraiment pas bien,
Quand on n'est pas la Joconde,
D'en adopter le maintien
Pour induire en spleens tout bleus le pauv' monde.

# PIERROT PHRASES

I.

Those pools of your eyes, by rushes enclosed,
O valiant leisurely lady,
When will they send back to me
The rising Moon of my beautiful soul?

It's been nearly an hour that langorously
My so simple heart has fed
On you, so rigorously hard,
With the honest eyes of a Saint Bernard.

Ah! Madam, it's most unfair of you,
Being so far from Mona Lisa,
To imitate her as you do,
And make the whole world's mood turn blue.

IX.

Ton geste,
Houri,
M'a l'air d'un memento mori
Qui signifie au fond: va, reste . . .

Mais, je te dirai ce que c'est,
Et pourquoi je pars, foi d'honnête
Poète
Français.

Ton cœur a la conscience nette,
Le mien n'est qu'un individu
Perdu
De dettes.

IX.

Your display,
Houri,
Looks like a memento mori
Meaning: go, or stay . . .

But, just so you'll know it,
And why I'm leaving, believe
A French
Poet:

Your heart has no regrets;
Mine is only a character
Lost
In debts.

X.

Que loin l'âme type
Qui m'a dit adieu
Parce que mes yeux
Manquaient de principes!

Elle, en ce moment,
Elle, si pain tendre,
Oh! peut-être engendre
Quelque garnement.

Car on l'a unie
Avec un monsieur,
Ce qu'il y a de mieux,
Mais pauvre en génie.

X.

That not-uncommon soul
Who said farewell to me
Just because my eyes
Lacked morality!

She was like warm fresh bread.
And now, imagine that!
May have been brought to bed
Giving birth to some brat.

For she was wed
As they all saw fit:
He was rich and well bred—
No charm, no wit.

XVI.

Je ne suis qu'un viveur lunaire
Qui fait des ronds dans les bassins,
Et cela, sans autre dessein
Que devenir un légendaire.

Retroussant d'un air de défi
Mes manches de mandarin pâle,
J'arrondis ma bouche et j'exhale
Des conseils doux de Crucifix.

Ah! oui, devenir légendaire,
Au seuil des siècles charlatans!
Mais où sont les Lunes d'antan?
Et que Dieu n'est-il à refaire?

XVI.

I'm only a playboy of the moon,
Making circles on park lagoons,
And that to all designs contrary,
Save for becoming legendary.

Pulling back with menacing pride
My sleeves, pale mandarin,
My mouth grows round, and I exhale
Sweet counsels of the Crucified.

Ah yes! to become a legend, here
On the threshold of charlatan ages!
But where are the Moons of Yesteryear?
Is there a God still worth His wages?

## DIALOGUE
## AVANT LE LEVER DE LA LUNE

—Je veux bien vivre; mais vraiment,
L'Idéal est trop élastique!

—C'est l'Idéal, son nom l'implique,
Hors son non-sens, le verbe ment.

Mais, tout est conteste; les livres
S'accouchent, s'entretuent sans lois!

—Certes! l'Absolu perd ses droits,
Là, où le Vrai consiste à vivre.

—Et, si j'amène pavillon
Et repasse au Néant ma charge?

—L'Infini, qui souffle du large,
Dit: "Pas de bêtises, voyons!"

—Ces chantiers du Possible ululent
A l'Inconcevable, pourtant!

—Un degré, comme il en est tant
Entre l'aube et le crépuscule.

—Etre actuel, est-ce, du moins,
Être adéquat à Quelque Chose?

—Conséquemment, comme la rose
Est nécessaire à ses besoins.

# DIALOGUE
# BEFORE MOONRISE

—I'd just as soon live, but really
The Ideal is too elasticized!

—It's the Ideal, as its name implies,
Aside from its non-sense, the word lies.

—But it's all disputed; the books
Give birth and kill each other at will!

—Of course! the Absolute's rights are nil
As long as the Truth consists of living.

—And if I haul down my flag,
Hand back to Nothingness my keys?

—The Infinite, blowing in from high seas,
Cries, "Take it easy, over there!"

—The workshops of the Possible swear
At the Inconceivable, nevertheless!

—What's one degree, more or less,
Between the twilight and the dawn?

—To be here and now, is it, at least,
To be for Something more than pose?

—In consequence, as the rose
Is necessary to its needs.

—Façon de dire peu commune
Que Tout est cercles vicieux?

Vicieux, mais Tout!
                              —J'aime mieux
Donc m'en aller selon la Lune.

—So, in your fashion, you infer
That All to vicious circles is tuned?

—Vicious, yes, All!
                                —I prefer
In that case to leave and follow the Moon.

# LITANIES
# DES DERNIERS QUARTIERS DE LA LUNE

Eucharistie
De l'Arcadie,

Qui fait de l'œil
Aux cœurs en deuil,

Ciel des idylles
Qu'on veut stériles,

Fonts baptismaux
Des blancs pierrots,

Dernier ciboire
De notre histoire,

Vortex-nombril
Du Tout-Nihil,

Miroir et Bible
Des Impassibles,

Hôtel garni
De l'infini,

Sphinx et Joconde
Des défunts mondes,

O Chanaan
Du bon Néant,

# LITANIES
# FOR THE LAST QUARTERS OF THE MOON

Eucharist
Of Arcady

Who winks an eye
At hearts' outcry,

Heaven where revel
Must be sterile,

Fonts and chrism
For Pierrots' baptism,

Ultimate pyx
Of human epics,

Vortex-navel
Of the Nil,

Mirror and Missal
For the Impassible,

Hotel equipped
With the Infinite,

Gioconda and Sphinx
Of worlds extinct,

O Canaan, tryst
With the good Abyss,

Néant, La Mecque
Des bibliothèques,

Léthé, Lotos,
*Exaudi nos!*

Our libraries'
Holy destiny,

Lethe, Lotus,
*Exaudi nos!*

from

# *DES FLEURS DE BONNE VOLONTÉ*

## RIGUEURS À NULLE AUTRE PAREILLES

Dans un album
Mourait fossile
Un géranium
Cueilli aux Iles.

Un fin Jongleur
En vieil ivoire
Raillait la fleur
Et ses histoires . . .

—"Un requiem!"
Demandait-elle.
"Vous n'aurez rien,
Mademoiselle!"

# RIGORS LIKE NONE OTHER

In an album,
Almost a ghost,
A geranium
Picked on the Coast.

A Troubadour,
Suave in ivory,
Laughed at the flower's
Tales of glory . . .

"A requiem
Would please me well."
"Nothing for you,
Mademoiselle!"

## AVANT-DERNIER MOT

L'Espace?
—Mon Cœur
Y meurt
Sans traces . . .

En vérité, du haut des terrasses,
    Tout est bien sans cœur.

    La Femme?
    —J'en sors,
    La mort
    Dans l'âme . . .

En vérité, mieux ensemble on pâme
    Moins on est d'accord.

    Le Rêve?
    —C'est bon
    Quand on
    L'achève . . .

En vérité, la Vie est bien brève,
    Le Rêve bien long.

    Que faire
    Alors
    Du corps
    Qu'on gère?

En vérité, ô mes ans, que faire
    De ce riche corps?

# NEXT-TO-THE-LAST WORD

Space?
—My Heart
Dies there.
No trace . . .

In fact, from up on a terrace,
What has a heart?

She?
—I get out
And see
Life's misery.

In fact, the better we swoon together
The less we agree.

Dreams?
—You win
When you do
Them in . . .

In fact, Life is so brief,
The Dream so long.

What's there
To do
With the flesh
In our care?

In fact, O my years, what to do
With this precious flesh?

Ceci,
Cela,
Par-ci
Par-là . . .

En vérité, en vérité, voilà.
Et pour le reste, que Tout m'ait en sa merci.

This
And that
Here
And there . . .

In fact, in fact, you see.
And for the rest, may All forgive me!

# DIMANCHES

> HAMLET: Have you a daughter?
> POLONIUS: I have, my lord.
> HAMLET: Let her not walk in the sun:
>   conception is a blessing; but not as
>   your daughter may conceive.

Le ciel pleut sans but, sans que rien l'émeuve,
Il pleut, il pleut, bergère! sur le fleuve . . .
Le fleuve a son repos dominical;
Pas un chaland, en amont, en aval.
Les Vêpres carillonnent sur la ville.
Les berges sont désertes, sans idylles.
Passe un pensionnat (ô pauvres chairs!)
Plusieurs ont déjà leurs manchons d'hiver.
Une qui n'a ni manchon, ni fourrures
Fait, tout en gris, une pauvre figure.
Et la voilà qui s'échappe des rangs,
Et court! O mon Dieu, qu'est-ce qu'il lui prend?
Et elle va se jeter dans le fleuve.
Pas un batelier, pas un chien Terr'-Neuve.
Le crépuscule vient; le petit port
Allume ses feux. (Ah! connu, l'décor!).
La pluie continue à mouiller le fleuve,
Le ciel pleut sans but, sans que rien l'émeuve.

# SUNDAYS

> HAMLET: Have you a daughter?
> POLONIUS: I have, my lord.
> HAMLET: Let her not walk in the sun:
>     conception is a blessing; but not as
>     your daughter may conceive.

The sky aimlessly rains, by nothing moved,
It's raining, raining, shepherdess! on the river . . .
The river in its dominical dream;
Not a boat upstream or down.
Vespers carillon over the town,
Empty of idylls, deserted shores.
A boarding-school goes by (oh, sad young bodies!)
Some already in winter clothes.
One has neither muff nor fur;
All in gray, a sad little figure.
Look! she's breaking out of line,
And runs! Good Lord! What's the matter with her?
And she throws herself into the stream.
No boatman, no Newfoundland dog to be seen.
It's evening now. The little harbor
Puts on its lights (ah! in the usual groove).
The rain continues to dampen the river,
The sky aimlessly rains, by nothing moved.

# DIMANCHES

JAQUES: Motley's the only wear.


Ils enseignent
Que la nature se divise en trois règnes,
Et professent
Le perfectionnement de notre Espèce.


Ah! des canapés
Dans un val de Tempé!


Des contrées
Tempérées,
Et des gens
Indulgents
Qui pâturent
La Nature.
En janvier,
Des terriers
Où l'on s'aime
Sans système,
Des bassins
Noirs d'essaims
D'acrobates
Disparates
Qui patinent
En sourdine . . .


Ah! vous savez ces choses
Tout aussi bien que moi;
Je ne vois pas pourquoi
On veut que j'en recause.

# SUNDAYS

JAQUES: Motley's the only wear.

They decided
That nature into three kingdoms is divided,
    And elected
Our Species to be perfected.

    Ah! Thessalian
Divans!

    Bland
    Lands
    And benign
    Minds
    Making pastures
    Of Nature.
    In our January
    Burrows, we
    Romance
    Just by chance;
    There are pools
    Black with schools
    Of disparate
    Acrobats
    Flashing by
    On the sly . . .

Ah! You know these things
Just as well as I;
Must I speak of them again?
I really don't see why.

# THE FAERIE COUNCIL

# LE CONCILE FÉERIQUE

*Dramatis personae:*
LE MONSIEUR.    LE CHŒUR.
LA DAME.    UN ECHO.
Nuit d'Étoiles

LA DAME
Oh! quelle nuit d'étoiles! quelles saturnales!
Oh! mais des galas inconnus
Dans les annales
Sidérales!

LE CHŒUR
Bref, un ciel absolument nu.

LE MONSIEUR
O Loi du rythme sans appel,
Le moindre astre te certifie,
Par son humble chorégraphie!
Mais, nul Spectateur éternel . . .
Ah! la terre humanitaire
N'en est pas moins terre-à-terre!
Au contraire.

LE CHŒUR
La terre, elle est ronde
Comme un pot-au-feu;
C'est un bien pauv' monde
Dans l'infini bleu.

LE MONSIEUR
Cinq sens seulement, cinq ressorts pour nos essors,
Ah! ce n'est pas un sort!
Quand donc nos cœurs s'en iront-ils en huit ressorts?

# THE FAERIE COUNCIL

*Dramatis personae:*

THE GENTLEMAN  THE CHORUS
THE LADY   AN ECHO
  Starry Night

THE LADY

Oh! what a starry night! A saturnalia!
  Oh! but the galas of magnitude
   Unknown! among the sidereal
    Paraphernalia.

CHORUS

In short, the sky is perfectly nude.

THE GENTLEMAN

O Law of rhythm without appeal,
That the least of stars will reveal
By its humble choreography!
But no eternal One to See . . .
Ah! the humanitarian Earth
Is none the less down-to-earth!
  On the contrary.

CHORUS

The Earth is round
Like a pot of stew,
A poor little world
In the infinite blue.

THE GENTLEMAN

Only five senses, five springs for all our soaring,
  Ah! a fate worse than boring!
And when will our hearts go away on eight springs?

Oh! le jour! quelle turne! . . .
J'en suis tout taciturne.

    LA DAME
    Oh! ces nuits sur les toits!
Je finirai bien par y prendre le froid . . .

    LE MONSIEUR
    Tiens, la Terre,
    Va te faire
    Très lan laire.

    LE CHŒUR
    Hé! pas choisi
    D'y naître, et hommes;
    Mais nous y sommes,
    Tenons-nous-y!
Écoutez mes enfants!—"Ah! mourir! mais me tordre,
"Dans l'orbe d'un exécutant de premier ordre!"
Rêve la Terre, sous la vessie de saindoux
De la lune laissant fuir un air par trop doux,
Vers les zéniths de brasiers de la voie lactée
(Autrement beaux, ce soir, que des lois constatées!)
Juillet a dégainé! Touristes des beaux yeux,
Quels jubés de bonheur échafaudent ces cieux,
Semis de pollens d'étoiles, manne divine,
Qu'éparpille le Bon Pasteur à ses gallines . . .

    LE MONSIEUR
Et puis le vent s'est tant surmené l'autre nuit . . .

    LA DAME
Et demain est si loin . . .

Oh! the day's a living tomb! . . .
I'm speechless with gloom.

>     THE LADY
> Oh! when these nights on the roof are all told,
> I'll certainly have a cold . . .

>     THE GENTLEMAN
> Oh, what a dearth
> Of you, Earth,
> Would be worth!

>     CHORUS
> Hey! didn't decide
> To be born here, and men;
> But now we've arrived,
> Let's stay till the end!

My children, listen! "Ah! to die! But to twist in this corner,
Bound to the orb of a first-class performer! . . ."
The Earth dreams, under a lard-bladder moon
Cleaving the too soft air to stray
Toward those blazing zeniths, the Milky Way
(Beautiful, this evening, outside the established order!).
July has unsheathed! Tourists with beautiful eyes,
What rood-screens of happiness scaffold the skies,
Seeded with star-pollen, manna divine
On which the Good Shepherd's chickens dine . . .

>     THE GENTLEMAN
> And the wind was so much overworked the other night . . .

>     THE LADY
> And tomorrow is so far away . . .

LE MONSIEUR
>Et ça souffre aujourd'hui.

Ah! pourrir!

LE CHŒUR
>Et la lune même (cette amie)

Salive et larmoie en purulente ophtalmie.
Et voici que des bleus sous-bois ont miaulé
Les mille nymphes; et (qu'est-ce que vous voulez)
Aussitôt mille touristes des yeux las rôdent,
Tremblants mais le cœur harnaché d'âpres méthodes!
Et l'on va. Et les uns connaissent des sentiers,
Qu'embaument de trois mois des fleurs d'abricotiers;
Et les autres, des parcs où la petite flûte
De l'oiseau bleu promet de si frêles rechutes;

L'ÉCHO

Oh! ces lunaires oiseaux bleus dont la chanson
Lunaire saura bien vous donner le frisson . . .

LE CHŒUR

Et d'autres, les terrasses pâles où le triste
Cor des paons réveillé fait que plus rien n'existe!
Et d'autres, les joncs des mares où le sanglot
Des reinettes vous tire maint sens mal éclos;
Et d'autres, les prés brûlés où l'on rampe; et d'autres
La Boue! où, semble-t-il, tout, avec nous se vautre!
Les capitales échauffantes, même au frais
Des grands hôtels tendus de pâles cuirs gaufrés,
Faussent; ah! mais ailleurs, aux grandes routes,
Au coin d'un bois mal famé,

L'ÉCHO
>Rien n'est aux écoutes . . .

THE GENTLEMAN
                And suffering today.
Ah! to decay!


THE CHORUS
        And even our old friend the moon
With purulent ophthalmia sobs and drools.
And now from the blue underbrush miaow
The thousand nymphs; and (naturally)
A thousand tourists are on the prowl,
Weary-eyed, faint, but methodical greed
At their hearts, they go. Some to known paths speed
Where three months are perfumed by apricot trees;
And others to parks where the little flute-calls
Of the bluebird promise such frail downfalls;


ECHO
Oh! those lunar bluebirds whose lunar trills
Can give you such chills . . .


CHORUS
For others, pale terraces where, awakened, the sad
Peacock's horn makes nothing more exist!
And for others, bulrushes in ponds where the sob
Of frogs draws from you many a hidden twist;
And others in burned meadows crawl,
Or the Mud! where all, it seems, with us must sprawl!
The torrid capitals, even if you stay
Cool in hotels lined pale with ornate leather,
Are off key; ah! but elsewhere, on the highway,
In a woodland corner evil loves,


ECHO
            The watch is away . . .

LE CHŒUR
Et celles dont le cœur gante six et demi,

L'ÉCHO
Et celles dont l'âme est gris perle,

LE CHŒUR
En bons amis,
Et d'un port panaché d'édénique opulence,
Vous brûlent leurs vaisseaux mondains vers des Enfances!

LE MONSIEUR
Oh! t'enchanter un peu la muqueuse du cœur!

LA DAME
Ah! vas-y; je n'ai plus rien à perdre à cet' heur';
La Terre est en plein air, et ma vie est gâchée;
Ne songe qu'à la Nuit, je ne suis point fâchée.

L'ÉCHO
Et la Vie et la Nuit font patte de velours.

LE CHŒUR
Se dépècent d'abord de grands quartiers d'amour:
Et lors, les chars de foin plein de bluets dévalent
Par les vallons des moissons équinoxiales . . .
O lointains balafrés de bleuâtres éclairs
De chaleur! puis il regrimperont, tous leurs nerfs
Tressés, vers l'hostie de la lune syrupeuse . . .

L'ÉCHO
Hélas! tout ça, c'est des histoires de muqueuses.

CHORUS
And ladies whose hearts wear size six-and-a-half gloves,

ECHO
And those whose souls are pearl gray,

CHORUS
As good friends,
And plumed with Eden-like opulence,
They burn for you worldly ships toward Innocence.

THE GENTLEMAN
Oh! to entertain your heart's mucosa!

THE LADY
Ah! I've no more to lose, so why don't you start?
The Earth's at large, and my life is torn apart;
Think only of Night; I'm well-disposed.

ECHO
And Life and the Night go on velvet paws.

CHORUS
Inaugurate the butcheries of love.
Then wagons with hay and flowers move from above
Through the valleys of equinoxial harvests . . .
O horizons gashed with lightning's bluish heat!
Then, with their nerves entwined, they'll retreat
Toward the Host of the syrupy moon . . .

ECHO
Alas, that same mucosa tune,

LE CHŒUR
Détraqué, dites-vous? Ah! par rapport à quoi?

L'ÉCHO
D'accord; mais le spleen vient, qui dit que l'on déchoit
Hors des fidélités noblement circonscrites.

LE CHŒUR
Mais le divin, chez nous, confond si bien les rites!

L'ÉCHO
Soit, mais mon spleen dit vrai, O langes des pudeurs,
C'est bien dans vos blancs plis tels quels qu'est le bonheur.

LE CHŒUR
Mais, au nom de Tout! on ne peut pas! la Nature
Nous rue à dénouer, dès janvier, leurs ceintures!

L'ÉCHO
Bon; si le spleen t'en dit, saccage universel!

LE CHŒUR
Vos êtres ont un sexe, et sont trop usuels,
Saccagez!

L'ÉCHO
      Ah! saignons, tandis qu'elles déballent
Leurs serres de beauté, pétale par pétale! . . .

LE CHŒUR
Les vignes de vos nerfs bourdonnent d'alcools noirs,
Enfants! ensanglantez la terre, ce pressoir
Sans planteur de justice!

CHORUS
Derailed, you say? Ah, from what line?

ECHO
Agreed; but bad moods arrive to say they decline
Outside of fidelities nobly circumscribed.

CHORUS
But our rites are so thoroughly twisted by the divine!

ECHO
Yes, but those moods are right. Oh, the linen of modesty holds
Happiness certain among its vague white folds.

CHORUS
But, in All's name! We can't! while Nature dictates
That from January on we unwrap their drapes!

ECHO
Right; if you must insist, then universal rape!

CHORUS
Your beings have a sex, and lack
Originality. Rape!

ECHO
         Ah! let's bleed while they unpack
Their greenhouses of beauty, petal by petal! . . .

CHORUS
The vines of your nerves are humming with black wine,
My children! stain the winepress earth with blood,
For no one plants justice!

## LE MONSIEUR ET LA DAME
Ah! tu m'aimes, je t'aime!
Que la mort ne nous ait qu'ivres-morts de nous-mêmes!

*Silence; nuit d'étoiles.—L'aube.*

## LE MONSIEUR,
*déclamant.*
La femme, mûre ou jeune fille,
J'en ai frôlé toutes les sortes,
Des faciles, des difficiles,
C'est leur mot d'ordre que j'apporte!
Des fleurs de chair, bien ou mal mises,
Des airs fiers ou seuls, selon l'heure;
Nul cri sur elles n'a de prise;
Nous les aimons, elle demeure.
Rien ne les tient, rien ne les fâche;
Elles veulent qu'on les trouv' belles,
Qu'on le leur râle et leur rabâche,
Et qu'on les use comme telles
Sans souci de serments, de bagues,
Suçons le peu qu'elles nous donnent;
Notre respect peut être vague:
Les yeux son haut et monotones.
Cueillons sans espoir et sans drame;
La chair vieillit après les roses;
Ah! parcourons le plus de gammes!
Vrai, il n'y a pas autre chose.

## LA DAME,
*déclamant à son tour.*

Si mon air vous dit quelque chose,
Vous auriez tort de vous gêner;

## THE LADY AND THE GENTLEMAN

Ah, you love me and I love you!
May death have us only dead-drunk on us two!

*Silence: starry night. The dawn.*

THE GENTLEMAN,
  *declaiming:*
As for women, young or ripe,
I've been up against every type
From the easy to the chaste;
And their own password here I've traced!
Flowers of flesh in assorted attire,
Proud or lonely airs as the hours inspire;
Not shackled they by cries of pain;
We love them, and she remains.
Not held or angered by our touch,
They want us to find them beautiful,
And rattle it to them, loud and dutiful,
And use them as such;
For vows and rings aren't worth very much.
Let's suck on the little they offer us,
Our respect can remain rather vague;
Their eyes are high and monotonous.
Let's pick without hope or theatrical poses;
The flesh grows old, but after the roses.
Ah! let's run over all the scales!
It's true that all else fails.

THE LADY,
  *declaiming in her turn:*

If you find my looks appealing,
Why be fearful? why be slow?

Je ne la fais pas à la pose.
Je suis la Femme, on me connaît.
Bandeaux plats ou crinière folle?
Dites? quel front vous rendrait fous?
J'ai l'art de toutes les écoles,
J'ai des âmes pour tous les goûts.
Cueillez la fleur de mes visages,
Sucez ma bouche et non ma voix,
Et n'en cherchez pas davantage,
Nul n'y vit clair, pas même moi.
Nos armes ne sont pas égales,
Pour que je vous tende la main:
Vous n'êtes que de braves mâles,
Je suis l'Éternel Féminin! . . .
Mon but se perd dans les étoiles! . . .
C'est moi qui suis la grande Isis! . . .
Nul ne m'a retroussé mon voile! . . .
Ne songez qu'à mes oasis.
Si mon air vous dit quelque chose,
Vous auriez tort de vous gêner:
Je ne la fais pas à la pose;
Je suis la Femme! on me connaît.

LE CHŒUR
  Touchant accord!
  Joli motif
  Décoratif,
  Avant la mort!
  Lui, nerveux,
  Qui se penche
Vers sa compagne aux larges hanches,
Aux longs caressables cheveux.
Car, l'on a beau baver les plus fières salives,
Leurs yeux sont tout! Ils rêvent d'aumônes furtives!

They are candidly revealing:
I am Woman, don't you know?
Shining braids or tangled locks -
Say what style tempts you to haste.
I know the arts of every school,
I have souls for every taste.
Pick the flower of my faces,
Suck my mouth and not my voice;
And don't ask for further graces . . .
None see clearly here, nor I.
We don't fight with equal weapons,
Why should I invite you in?
You are only guileless males,
I, the Eternal Feminine! . . .
My goal is lost among the stars! . . .
I'm the elemental Isis! . . .
No one has drawn back my veil! . . .
Keep your dreams for my oases.
If you find my looks appealing,
Why be fearful? why be slow?
They are candidly revealing:
I am Woman! don't you know?

CHORUS
    A touching accord!
    Decorative
    Pretty motif,
    While we still live!
    He, nervously,
    Leans
    Toward his friend with the heavy hips
    And the long caressable hair.
For in spite of proudly salivating lips,
Their eyes are everything! They dream of furtive alms!

O chairs d'humains, ciboire du bonheur! on peut
Blaguer, la paire est là, comme un et un font deux.
—Mais, ces yeux, plus on va, se fardent de mystère!
—Et bien, travaillez à les ramener sur terre!
—Ah! la chasteté n'est en fleur qu'en souvenir!
—Mais ceux qui l'ont cueillie en renaissent martyrs!
Martyrs mutuels! de frère à sœur sans père!
Comment ne voit-on pas que c'est là notre Terre?
Et qu'il n'y a que ça! que le reste est impôts
Dont vous n'avez pas même à chercher l'à-propos!
Il faut répéter ces choses! Il faut qu'on tette
Ces choses! Jusqu'à ce que la Terre se mette,
Voyant enfin que tout vivote sans témoin,
A vivre aussi pour elle, et dans son petit coin!

LA DAME
La pauvre Terre, elle est si bonne! . . .

LE MONSIEUR
Oh! désormais, je m'y cramponne.

LA DAME
De tous nos bonheurs d'autochtones!

LE MONSIEUR
Tu te pâmes, je m'y vautre!

LE CHŒUR
Consolez-vous les uns les autres.

O human flesh! pyx of happiness! Easy to
Joke, but the pair is there, as one and one make two.
—But those eyes, further on, are painted with mystery!
Then work at bringing them back again to earth!
—Ah! only in memory flowers chastity!
For those who gathered it, martyrdom! rebirth
As mutual martyrs, from brother to sister, fatherless!
Why don't you see that that is truly our Earth!
And all there is! and the rest is nothing but tax
About which you might just as well relax!
These things must be repeated! Sucked in
At the breast! until at last the Earth begins,
Seeing that all struggles on while no one cares,
To live in its little corner, minding its own affairs!

> THE LADY
> The poor Earth tries so hard to please! . . .

> THE GENTLEMAN
> Oh! from now on I'm set to follow!

> THE LADY
> The pleasures of aborigines!

> THE GENTLEMAN
> While you swoon, I'll wallow!

> CHORUS
> Console yourselves, one and all.

# DERNIER VERS

# DERNIERS VERS

## I.
## L'HIVER QUI VIENT

Blocus sentimental! Messageries du Levant! . . .
Oh! tombée de la pluie! Oh! tombée de la nuit,
Oh! le vent! . . .
La Toussaint, La Noël, et la Nouvelle Année,
Oh! dans les bruines, toutes mes cheminées! . . .
D'usines . . .

On ne peut plus s'asseoir, tous les bancs sont mouillés;
Crois-moi, c'est bien fini jusqu'à l'année prochaine,
Tous les bancs sont mouillés, tant les bois sont rouillés,
Et tant les cors ont fait ton ton, ont fait ton taine! . . .

Ah! nuées accourues des côtes de la Manche,
Vous nous avez gâté notre dernier dimanche.

Il bruine;
Dans la forêt mouillée, les toiles d'araignées
Ploient sous les gouttes d'eau, et c'est leur ruine.
Soleils plénipotentiares des travaux en blonds Pactoles
Des spectacles agricoles,
Où êtes-vous ensevelis?
Ce soir un soleil fichu gît au haut du coteau,
Gît sur le flanc, dans les genêts, sur son manteau.
Un soleil blanc comme un crachat d'estaminet
Sur un litière de jaunes genêts,
De jaunes genêts d'automne.
Et les cors lui sonnent!
Qu'il revienne . . .
Qu'il revienne à lui!

# LAST POEMS

## I.

## THE COMING WINTER

Sentimental Blockade! Express from the rising Sun! . . .
Oh! falling rain, oh! nightfall,
Oh! the wind . . .
All Saints' Day, Christmas, the New Year,
Oh, in the drizzle, all my fine chimneys! . . .
Of factories . . .

There's nowhere to sit down, all the benches are wet;
Believe me, it's all over once again,
All the benches are wet, the wood is so rusty,
And so many horns have sounded *ton ton*, have sounded *ton taine!* . . .

Ah! storm clouds rushed from the Channel's coast,
You can boast of spoiling the last of our Sundays.

Drizzle;
In the wet fields, the spiderwebs
Give way to the waterdrops, and fizzle.
Plenipotentiary suns of blond river gold-mines,
Of agricultural pantomimes,
Where is your tomb?
This evening a worn-out sun lies dead on top of the hill,
Lies on his side, in the broom, on his coat.
A sun white as tavern spit
On a litter of golden broom,
The yellow autumnal broom.
And the horns resound!
Calling him . . .
Calling him back to himself!

Taïaut! Taïaut! et hallali!
O triste antienne, as-tu fini! . . .
Et font les fous! . . .
Et il gît là, comme une glande arachée dans un cou,
Et il frissonne, sans personne! . . .

Allons, allons, et hallali!
C'est l'Hiver bien connu qui s'amène;
Oh! les tournants des grandes routes,
Et sans petit Chaperon Rouge qui chemine! . . .
Oh! leurs ornières des chars de l'autre mois,
Montant en don quichottesques rails
Vers les patrouilles des nuées en déroute
Que le vent malmène vers les transatlantiques bercails! . . .
Accélérons, accélérons, c'est la saison bien connu, cette fois.

Et le vent, cette nuit, il en a fait de belles!
O dégâts, ô nids, ô modestes jardinets!
Mon cœur et mon sommeil: ô échos des cognées! . . .

Tous ces rameaux avaient encor leurs feuilles vertes,
Les sous-bois ne sont plus qu'un fumier de feuilles mortes;
Feuilles, folioles, qu'on bon vent vous emporte
Vers les étangs par ribambelles,
Ou pour le feu du garde-chasse,
Ou les sommiers des ambulances
Pour les soldats loin de la France.

C'est la saison, c'est la saison, la rouille envahit les masses,
La rouille ronge en leurs spleens kilométriques
Les fils télégraphiques des grandes routes où nul ne passe.

Les cors, les cors, les cors—mélancoliques! . . .
Mélancoliques! . . .

*Taiaut! Taiaut!* and *hallali!*
O doleful anthem, when will you die! . . .
And madly they have fun . . .
And he lies there like a gland torn from a neck,
Shivering, without anyone! . . .

On, on, and *hallali!*
In the lead is Winter, that's understood;
Oh! the turns in the highways,
And without the wandering Little Red Riding Hood!
Oh! their ruts from last month's cars,
Trails in a Don Quixotic climb
Toward the routed cloud patrols
That the wind mauls toward transatlantic folds! . . .
Accelerate, accelerate, it's the well-known season, this time.

And the wind, last night, really put on a show!
O havoc, O nests, O diffident gardens!
My heart and my sleep: O echoes of ax-blows! . . .

All those branches had their green leaves still,
Now the underbrush, only a mulch of dead leaves;
Leaves, leaflets, may a good wind's will
Race you off in swarms toward ponds,
Or for the game warden's fireplace,
Or for ambulance mattresses
For soldiers far away from France.

It's the season, the season; rust invades the masses,
Rust gnaws the kilometric spleens
Of telegraph wires on highways no one passes.

The horns, the horns, the horns—melancholy! . . .
Melancholy! . . .

S'en vont, changeant de ton,
Changeant de ton et de musique,
Ton ton, ton taine, ton ton! . . .
Les cors, les cors, les cors! . . .
S'en sont allés au vent du Nord.

Je ne puis quitter ce ton: que d'échos! . . .
C'est la saison, c'est la saison, adieu vendanges! . . .
Voici venir les pluies d'une patience d'ange.
Adieu vendanges, et adieu tous les paniers,
Tous les paniers Watteau des bourrées sous les marronniers.
C'est la toux dans les dortoirs du lycée qui rentre,
C'est la tisane sans le foyer,
La phtisie pulmonaire attristant le quartier,
Et toute la misère des grands centres.

Mais, lainages, caoutchoucs, pharmacie, rêve,
Rideaux écartés du haut des balcons des grèves
Devant l'océan de toitures des faubourgs,
Lampes, estampes, thé, petits-fours,
Serez-vous pas mes seules amours! . . .
(Oh! et puis, es-ce que tu connais, outre les pianos,
Le sobre et vespéral mystère hebdomadaire
Des statistiques sanitaires
Dans les journaux?)

Non, non! c'est la saison et la planète falote!
Que l'autan, que l'autan
Effiloche les savates que le Temps se tricote!
C'est la saison, oh déchirements! c'est la saison!
Tous les ans, tous les ans,
J'essaierai en chœur d'en donner la note.

Go away, changing their tone,
Changing their tone and their tune,
*Ton ton, ton taine, ton ton!* . . .
The horns, the horns, the horns! . . .
Have gone away to the North Wind.

I can't get out of this echoing tone . . .
It's the season, the season, farewell grape harvests! . . .
Now, with a patience of angels, come the rains;
Farewell harvests, baskets, nothing remains,
Those Watteau baskets under the chestnut trees.
It's the cough in dormitories coming back,
Herb-tea without a hearth,
Pneumonias grieving the neighborhood,
And all the metropolitan miseries.

But wool clothes, rubbers, pharmacies, dreams,
Curtains drawn back from high balconies
Facing suburban roofs like a sea,
Prints, lamps, cakes and tea,
Won't I have only you to love! . . .
(Oh! and then, do you know, apart from the pianos,
Each week, austere twilight mystery,
The journalistic
Vital statistics?)

No, no! it's the season; the planet repines!
May the storm, the storm
Unravel the slippers knitted by Time!
It's the season, O rendings! the season!
And every year, every year
I'll try in chorus to sound its rhyme.

## II.
## LE MYSTÈRE DES TROIS CORS

Un cor dans la plaine
Souffle à perdre haleine,
Un autre, du fond des bois,
Lui répond;
L'un chante ton taine
Aux forêts prochaines,
Et l'autre ton ton
Aux échos des monts.

Celui de la plaine
Sent gonfler ses veines,
Ses veines du front;
Celui du bocage,
En vérité, ménage
Ses jolis poumons.

—Où donc tu te caches,
Mon beau cor de chasse?
Que tu es méchant!

—Je cherche ma belle,
Là-bas qui m'appelle
Pour voir le Soleil couchant.

—Taïaut! Taïaut! Je t'aime!
Hallali! Roncevaux!

—Etre aimé est bien doux;
Mais, le Soleil qui se meurt, avant tout!

Le soleil dépose sa pontificale étole,
Lâche les écluses du Grand-Collecteur

## II.
## THE MYSTERY OF THE THREE HORNS

A horn in the plain
Blew a high strain,
Another, deep in the wood
Understood;
The first sang *ton taine*
To the woods from the plain,
And the other *ton ton*
To the echoing mountain.

He in the plain
Feels his veins swelling,
His forehead veins;
The other likes best
It seems, to rest
His dainty chest.

"Where are you hiding,
My fine hunting horn?
Your silence is wrong!"

"I seek my lady
Down there calling me
To see the setting Sun."

*"Taiautl Taiaut!* I love you!
*Hallali! Roncevaux!"*

"It's sweet enough to be loved,
But the dying Sun stands above!"

The sun lays down his pontifical stole,
Opens the locks of the Great Water-hole

En mille Pactoles
Que les plus artistes
De nos liquoristes
Attisent de cent fioles de vitriol oriental! . . .
Le sanglant étang, aussitôt s'étend, aussitôt s'étale,
Noyant les cavales du quadrige
Qui se cabre, et qui patauge, et puis se fige
Dans ces déluges de Bengale et d'alcool! . . .


Mais les durs sables et les cendres de l'horizon
Ont vite bu tout cet étalage de poisons.


Ton ton ton taine, les gloires! . . .


Et les cors consternés
Se retrouvent nez à nez;


Ils sont trois;
Le vent se lève, il commence à faire froid.


Ton ton ton taine, les gloires!


—Bras dessus, bras dessous,
"Avant de rentrer chacun chez nous,
"Si nous allions boire
"Un coup?"


Pauvres cors! pauvres cors!
Comme ils dirent cela avec un rire amer!
(Je les entends encor.)


Le lendemain, l'hôtesse du *Grand-Saint-Hubert*
Les trouva tous trois morts.

Into a thousand rivers of gold
That the artists
Among our alchemists
Fire with a hundred phials of oriental vitriol! . . .
Bleeding, the pond instantly stretches, instantly spreads,
Drowning the Chariot's four-abreast
Who rearing and plunging are fixed
In floods of blue fire and alcohol! . . .

But the hard sands and ashes of the horizon
Have quickly drunk all that display of poison.

*Ton ton ton taine*, for glory! . . .

And the horns, amazed
Find themselves face to face;

They are three, all told;
The wind rises; it's beginning to be cold.

*Ton ton ton taine*, for glory!

Arm in arm, arm in arm:
"Before we go home, do you think
There would be any harm
In a drink?"

Poor horns, poor horns!
With a bitter laugh it was said!
(I hear them once more.)

In the morning the hostess at Saint Hubert's Inn
Found all three of them dead.

On fut quérir les autorités
De la localité,

Qui dressèrent procès-verbal
De ce mystère très immoral.

They sent for the authorities
Of the locality,

Who investigated the history
Of this very immoral mystery.

## III.
## DIMANCHES

Bref, j'allais me donner d'un "Je vous aime"
Quand je m'avisai non sans peine
Que d'abord je ne me possédais pas bien moi-même.

(Mon Moi, c'est Galathée aveuglant Pygmalion!
Impossible de modifier cette situation.)

Ainsi donc, pauvre, pâle et piètre individu
Qui ne croit à son Moi qu'à ses moments perdus,
Je vis s'effacer ma fiancée
Emportée par le cours des choses,
Telle l'épine voit s'effeuiller,
Sous prétexte de soir sa meilleure rose.

Or, cette nuit anniversaire, toutes les Walkyries du vent
Sont revenues beugler par les fentes de ma porte:
*Vae soli!*
Mais, ah! qu'importe?
Il fallait m'en étourdir avant!
Trop tard! ma petite folie est morte!
Qu'importe *Vae soli!*
Je ne retrouverai plus ma petite folie.

Le grand vent bâillonné,
S'endimanche enfin le ciel du matin.
Et alors, eh! allez donc, carillonnez,
Toutes cloches des bons dimanches!
Et passez layettes et collerettes et robes blanches
Dans un frou-frou de lavandes et de thym
Vers l'encens et les brioches!
Tout pour la famille, quoi! *Vae soli!* C'est certain.

## III.
## SUNDAYS

To give myself to an "I love you!" I was all set,
When I realized, with regret,
That myself wasn't quite in hand as yet.

(My self is Galatea blinding Pygmalion!
Impossible to modify that situation.)

And so, poor, wan and paltry—true
I believe in Me, (when I've nothing else to do)
I saw my fiancée drift away,
Carried off as the fates dispose,
Like the thorn that sees the petals
Falling, by evening excused, from its best rose.

Then, that anniversary night when all the wind Valkyries
Came back to bellow through cracks in my door:
*Vae soli!*
But, ah! who cares?
That should have drowned my sorrows long before!
Too late! My little folly is dead!
Who cares about *Vae soli?*
Forever has my little folly fled.

Once the great wind is gagged,
The morning sky at last puts on its Sunday best.
And then, eh! go on, chime
All you good Sunday bells!
And put on layettes, collarettes, a white dress,
In a rustle of lavender and thyme
Toward incense and breakfast!
What the family wants it gets! *(Vae soli.)*

La jeune demoiselle à l'ivoirin paroissien
Modestement rentre au logis.
On le voit, son petit corps bien reblanchi
Sait qu'il appartient
A un tout autre passé que le mien!

Mon corps, ô ma sœur, a bien mal à sa belle âme . . .

Oh! voilà que ton piano
Me recommence, si natal maintenant!
Et ton cœur qui s'ignore s'y ânonne
En ritournelles de bastringues à tout venant,
Et ta pauvre chair s'y fait mal! . . .
A moi, Walkyries!
Walkyries des hypocondries et des tueries!

Ah! que je te les tordrais avec plaisir,
Ce corps bijou, ce cœur à ténor,
Et te dirais leur fait, et puis encore
La manière de s'en servir
De s'en servir à deux,
Si tu voulais seulement m'approfondir ensuite un peu!

Non, non! C'est sucer la chair d'un cœur élu,
Adorer d'incurables organes
S'entrevoir avant que les tissus se fanent
En monomanes, en reclus!

Et ce n'est pas sa chair qui me serait tout.
Et je ne serais pas qu'un grand cœur pour elle,
Mais quoi s'en aller faire les fous
Dans des histoires fraternelles!
L'âme et la chair, la chair et l'âme,

The young lady with the ivory-colored missal
Returns to her lodgings, modestly.
It's clear her little well-rewhitened body
Knows that it belongs
To a past quite separate from mine!

My body, O sister, hurts in its beautiful soul . . .

Oh! there's your piano
Beginning me again, so natal now!
And your heart's whole ignorance stutters out
In bar room tunes to anyone
And grates on your poor flesh! . . .
To me, Valkyries!
Valkyries of hypochondrias, butcheries!

Ah! with what pleasure I'd twist
That jewel of a body, that tenor's heart,
And tell them what they are, and what's more,
The way to use it,
To use it for two,
If after that you'd just investigate me a bit!

No, no! to suck on the flesh of a chosen heart,
To adore incurable organs,
A glimpse of each other before that interlude
Fades to a monomoniacal solitude.

And it isn't her flesh that would be all for me.
And I wouldn't be just a noble heart for her;
But to go and make fools of ourselves
Over some brotherly history!
The soul and the flesh, the flesh and soul

C'est l'esprit édénique et fier
D'être un peu l'Homme avec la Femme.

En attendant, oh! garde-toi des coups de tête,
Oh! file ton rouet et prie et reste honnête.

—Allons, dernier des poètes,
Toujours enfermé tu te rendras malade!
Vois, il fait beau temps, tout le monde est dehors,
Va donc acheter deux sous d'ellébore
Ça te fera une petite promenade.

That's the Eden-like spirit, proud
Of being something like Man with Her.

In the meantime, oh! don't do anything in haste,
Oh! just spin your wheel, and pray, and be chaste.

—Come on, least of poets,
You'll be sick if you spend all your time indoors!
Look, it's a lovely day, everyone's outside,
Go buy a penny's worth of hellebore,
It'll give you a little walk.

## IV.
## DIMANCHES

C'est l'automne, l'automne, l'automne,
Le grand vent et toute sa séquelle
De représailles! et de musiques! . . .
Rideaux tirés, clôture annuelle,
Chute des feuilles, des Antigones, des Philomèles:
Mon fossoyeur, *Alas poor Yorick!*
Les remue à la pelle! . . .

Vivent l'Amour et les feux de paille! . . .
Les Jeunes Filles inviolables et frêles
Descendent vers la petite chapelle
Dont les chimériques cloches
Du joli, joli dimanche
Hygiéniquement et élégamment les appellent.

Comme tout se fait propre autour d'elles!
Comme tout en est dimanche!

Comme on se fait dur et boudeur à leur approche! . . .
Ah! moi, je demeure l'Ours Blanc!
Je suis venu par ces banquises
Plus pures que les communiantes en blanc . . .
Moi, je ne vais pas à l'église,
Moi je suis le Grand Chancelier de l'Analyse,
Qu'on se le dise.

Pourtant! pourtant! Qu'est-ce que c'est que cette anémie?
Voyons, confiez vos chagrins à votre vieil ami . . .

## IV.

## SUNDAYS

It's autumn, autumn, autumn,
The great wind and all its string
Of reprisals! and music! . . ,
Drawn curtains, closed for the season,
Leaves, Antigones, Philomelas, falling;
My gravedigger, *Alas poor Yorick!*
Stirring them, shoveling . . . !

Long live Love and straw fires!
Inviolable and frail, the Young Ladies
Go down toward the chapel
Whose chimerical bells
Of cheerful, cheerful Sunday
Call them, hygienically, elegantly.

Close to them it all becomes so clean!
And all so Sunday!

How hard we grow, and sulky, when they near! . . .
Ah! I'm still the Polar Bear!
I came here via the ice-floes
Purer than white Communion robes;
And never go to church.
For I'm the Grand Chancellor of Analysis,
Remember this.

But just the same! Why be so anemic?
Come tell your troubles to an old friend . . .

Vraiment! Vraiment!
Ah! Je me tourne vers la mer, les éléments
Et tout ce qui n'a plus que les noirs grognements!

Oh! que c'est sacré!
Et qu'il y faut de grandes veillées!

Pauvre, pauvre, sous couleur d'attraits! . . .

Et nous, et nous,
Ivres, ivres, avant qu'émerveillés . . .
Qu'émerveillés et à genoux! . . .

Et voyez comme on tremble,
Au premier grand soir
Que tout pousse au désespoir
D'en mourir ensemble!

O merveille qu'on n'a su que cacher!
Si pauvre et si brûlante et si martyre!
Et qu'on n'ose toucher
Qu'à l'aveugle, en divin délire!

O merveille.
Reste cachée, idéale violette,
L'Univers te veille,
Les générations de planètes te tettent,
De funérailles en relevailles! . . .

Oh! que c'est plus haut
Que ce Dieu et que la Pensée!
Et rien qu'avec ces chers yeux en haut,
Tout inconscients et couleur de pensée! . . .

Si frêle, si frêle!

Truly! Truly!
Ah! I turn to the sea, the elements,
And all that has nothing left but grumbling laments!

Oh, it's so holy!
And needing such lengthy care!

Poor, poor, camouflaged by charm! . . .

And we, and we,
Drunk, drunk before marveling . . .
Marveling, and on our knees! . . .

And see how we tremble so
At this first great evening
That we would, despairing,
Die of it all, together!

O marvel they could only conceal!
So poor and so burning, martyrdom!
And that they dare not touch
Save blindly in a divine delirium!

O marvel.
Stay hidden, ideal violet,
The Universe doesn't forget,
The generations of planets suckle you
From funerals to christenings! . . .

Oh! so high
Beyond this God and Thought!
And all only by those dear eyes on high,
Quite unknowing and the color of thought!

So frail, so frail!

Et tout le mortel foyer
Tout, tout ce foyer en elle! . . .

Oh, pardonnez-lui si, malgré elle,
Et cela tant lui sied,
Parfois ses prunelles clignent un peu
Pour vous demander un peu
De vous apitoyer un peu!

O frêle, frêle et toujours prête
Pour ces messes dont on a fait un jeu,
Penche, penche ta chère tête, va,
Regarde les grappes des premiers lilas,
Il ne s'agit pas de conquêtes, avec moi,
Mais d'au-delà!

Oh! puissions-nous quitter la vie
Ensemble dès cette Grand'Messe,
Écœurés de notre espèce
Qui baille assouvie
Dès le parvis! . . .

And all our mortal home
In her, all, all this home!

Oh, forgive her if, in spite of herself,
And it's really so becoming,
Sometimes her eyelashes flutter a little
Asking a little
Be softened a little!

O frail, frail, and always ready
For those Masses they've made a game,
Bow, bow your dear head, go,
Look at the blooms the lilacs grow,
Conquest is not my aim, you know,
But Beyond!

Ah, couldn't we leave this life,
Together right after this High Mass,
Sick of our species
Which yawns, replete
Back on the street! . . .

## V.

## PETITION

Amour absolu, carrefour sans fontaine;
Mais, à tous les bouts, d'étourdissantes fêtes foraines.

Jamais franches,
Ou le poing sur la hanche:
Avec toutes, l'amour s'échange
Simple et sans foi comme un bonjour.

O bouquets d'oranger cuirassés de satin,
Elle s'éteint, elle s'éteint,
La divine Rosace
A voir vos noces de sexes livrés à la grosse,
Courir en valsant vers la fosse
Commune! . . . Pauvre race!
Pas d'absolus; des compromis;
Tout est pas plus, tout est permis.

Et cependant, ô des nuits, laissez-moi Circés
Sombrement coiffées à la Titus,
Et les yeux en grand deuil comme des pensées!
Et passez,
Béatifiques Vénus
Etalées et découvrant vos gencives comme un régal,
Et bâillant des aisselles au soleil,
Dans l'assourdissement des cigales,
Ou, droites, tenant sur fond violet le lotus
Des sacrilèges domestiques,
En faisant de l'index: motus!

## V.
## PETITION

Absolute love, fountainless intersections
With carnavals blaring in all directions.

Truth from their lips?
No! just hands on hips.
From every one of them love comes your way,
Simple and from the heart, like "have a good day!"

Armored in satin, O orange-blossom bouquets!
The holy Rose Window
Fades, fades
From seeing marriages, sex delivered by the gross,
Racing in waltz-time toward a common
Grave! . . . Poor human race!
No absolute; just compromise.
All within limits; no problems arise.

But still, some nights, you Circes, please go your way,
With your hair coiffed in a somber Roman style,
And your mourning eyes like the dark heart of pansies,
Pass by, I say,
To each beatific Venus
Splayed out; exposed like a gift, her succulent gums,
Her armpits yawning toward the sun
In the deafening sound of cicadas!
Or, upright, with, on a purple ground, the lotus,
Forgetfulness, for conjugal sacrilege—
Against her lips a vertical finger: ssh!

Passez, passez, bien que les yeux vierges
Ne soient que cadrans d'émail bleu,
Marquant telle heure que l'on veut,
Sauf à garder pour eux, pour Elle,
Leur heure immortelle.
Sans doute au premier mot,
On va baisser les yeux,
Et peut-être choir en syncope,

On est si vierge a fleur de robe
Peut-être même à fleur de peau,
Mais leur destinée est bien interlope, au nom de Dieu!

O historiques esclaves!
Oh! leur petite chambre!
Qu'on peut les en faire descendre
Vers d'autres étages,
Vers le moins frélatées des caves,
Vers le moins ange-gardien des ménages!

Et alors, le grand Suicide, à froid,
Et leur amen d'une voix sans Elle,
Tout en vaquant aux petits soins secrets,
Et puis leur éternel air distrait
Leur grand air de dire: "De quoi?
"Ah! de quoi, au fond, s'il vous plaît?"

Mon Dieu, que l'idéal
La dépouillât de ce rôle d'ange!
Qu'elle adoptât l'Homme comme égal!
Oh, que ses yeux ne parlent plus Idéal,
Mais simplement d'humains échanges,
En frères et soeur par le coeur,
Et fiancés par le passé,
Et puis unis par l'Infini!

Pass by, pass by, although her innocent eyes
Are only clock-faces enameled blue,
Showing the hour you choose
Except the one for Them, for Her,
The one that's to be forever.
No doubt, as you begin to rhapsodize
She'll lower those eyes,
And might go so far as to faint,

So virgin on the surface,
And maybe even under the skin,
But dubious, my God, must be her fate!

O immemorial slaves!
Oh! their little rooms
From which they are led down,
And down, and so they go
Toward domestic degradation—
No guardian angels here below.

And then, crossing their fingers, they say Amen,
In a passionless Suicide,
But attending to their own secret vows.
That's why they look so preoccupied,
Always seeming to say,
"What now? Please! what now?"

If only the Ideal
Would extract her from her angel role,
Let her adopt Man as her equal!
Oh! If her eyes could stop speaking of the Ideal
And content themselves with human affairs,
Like brother and sister at heart,
Fiancés from childhood on,
Then united by the Infinite!

Oh, simplement d'infinis échanges
A la fin des journées
A quatre bras moissonnées,
Quand les tambours, quand les trompettes,
Ils s'en vont sonnant la retraite,
Et qu'on prend le frais sur le pas des portes,
En vidant les pots de grès
A la santé des années mortes
Qui n'ont pas laissé de regrets,
Au su de tout le canton
Que depuis toujours nous habitons,
Ton ton, ton taine, ton ton.

Oh, just endless conversations
At the end of the day,
Their arms around each other.
When the drums roll and the trumpets blow
The retreat, it's time to go home,
Time to sit outside on the doorstep
And drink a cup or two or three
To the health of the by-gone years
With nothing at all to regret
As far as anyone knows,
And we've lived in this place so long,
Ding dong, dong ding, ding dong.

## VI
### SIMPLE AGONIE

O paria!—Et revoici les sympathies de mai.
Mais tu ne peux que te répéter, ô honte!
Et tu te gonfles et ne crèves jamais.
Et tu sais fort bien, ô paria,
Que ce n'est pas du tout ça.

Oh! que
Devinant l'instant le plus seul de la nature,
Ma mélodie, toute et unique, monte,
Dans le soir et redouble, et fasse tout ce qu'elle peut
Et dise la chose qu'est la chose,
Et retombe, et reprenne,
Et fasse de la peine,
O solo de sanglots,
Et reprenne et retombe
Selon la tâche qui lui incombe.
Oh! que ma musique
Se crucifie,
Selon sa photographie
Accoudée et mélancolique! . . .

Il faut trouver d'autres thèmes,
Plus mortels et plus suprêmes.
Oh! bien, avec le monde tel quel,
Je vais me faire un monde plus mortel!

Les âmes y seront à musique,
Et tous les intérêts puérilement charnels,
O fanfares dans les soirs,
Ce sera barbare,
Ce sera sans espoir.

## VI
## SIMPLE AGONY

O pariah!—And once again the sympathies of May.
But you can only repeat yourself, O shame!
And you swell up and never give way.
And you know very well, O pariah,
That that's not it at all.

Oh! may
From nature divining that moment most alone,
My melody, all and unique, rise
Through the evening and grow, and do what it can
And say the thing which is the thing
And fall back and begin again,
And cause pain,
O solo despair,
And begin and fall again
As the weight of its task may require.
Oh! may my music at last
Be crucified
In accordance with her photograph,
Her head resting on her hands, and so sad! . . .

We'll have to find other themes
More mortal and supreme,
Oh, well! with this world at my call
I'll make myself a world more mortal!

The souls will be set to music
And all that matters childishly carnal,
O, in the evening, fanfares;
It will be barbaric,
It will be without hope.

Enquêtes, enquêtes,
Seront l'unique fête!
Qui m'en défie?
J'entasse sur mon lit, les journaux, linge sale,
Dessins de mode, photographies quelconques,
Toute la capitale,
Matrice sociale.

Que nul n'intercède,
Ce ne sera jamais assez,
Il n'y a qu'un remède,
C'est de tout casser.

O fanfares dans les soirs!
Ce sera barbare,
Ce sera sans espoir.
Et nous aurons beau la piétiner à l'envi,
Nous ne serons jamais plus cruels que la vie,
Qui fait qu'il est des animaux injustement rossés,
Et des femmes à jamais laides . . .
Que nul n'intercède,
Il faut tout casser.

Alléluia, Terre paria.
Ce sera sans espoir,
De l'aurore au soir,
Quand il n'y en aura plus il y en aura encore,
Du soir à l'aurore.
Alléluia, Terre paria!
Les hommes de l'art
Ont dit: "Vrai, c'est trop tard."
Pas de raison,
Pour ne pas activer sa crevaison.

Aux armes, citoyens! Il n'y a plus de RAISON:

Inquests, inquests
Will be the only festivals!
Who objects?
I pile on my bed newspapers, dirty underwear,
Fashion designs, assorted photographs,
All our capital,
The matrix of human society.

Let no protest be spoken,
It will never be enough,
There is only one cure that sticks,
All must be broken.

O, in the evening, fanfares!
It will be barbaric,
It will be without hope.
And even if we trample where we like,
Never will we be more cruel than life
Which makes there be animals unjustly beaten,
And women ugly forever . . .
Let no protest be spoken,
All must be broken.

Hallelujah, pariah Earth.
It will be without hope
From dawn to evening;
When there's no more it still won't be gone,
From evening to dawn.
Hallelujah, pariah Earth!
Artists of worth
Have said: "Yes, it's too late."
No reason
Not to help it go out of season.

*Aux armes, citoyens!* There's no more REASON:

Il prit froid l'autre automne,
S'étant attardé vers les peines des cors,
Sur la fin d'un beau jour.
Oh! ce fut pour vos cors, et ce fut pour l'automne,
Qu'il nous montra qu' "on meurt d'amour"!
On ne le verra plus aux fêtes nationales,
S'enfermer dans l'Histoire et tirer les verrous,
Il vint trop tôt, il est reparti sans scandale;
O vous qui m'écoutez, rentrez chacun chez vous.

He took cold the other autumn,
Having lingered toward the sorrows of horns
At the end of a lovely afternoon.
Oh! it was for your horns, and it was for autumn
That he showed us how to "die for love"!
We'll never see him again on national holidays
Close himself up in History, drawing the bolt.
He came too early, disturbing no one he went away;
O you who are listening to me, all of you, go home.

## VII
## SOLO DE LUNE

Je fume, étalé face au ciel,
Sur l'impériale de la diligence,
Ma carcasse est cahotée, mon âme danse
Comme un Ariel;
Sans miel, sans fiel, ma belle âme danse,
O routes, coteaux, ô fumées, ô vallons,
Ma belle âme, ah! récapitulons.

Nous nous aimions comme deux fous,
On s'est quitté sans en parler,
Un spleen me tenait exilé,
Et ce spleen me venait de tout. Bon.

Ses yeux disaient: "Comprenez-vous?
"Pourquoi ne comprenez-vous pas?"
Mais nul n'a voulu faire le premier pas,
Voulant trop tomber ensemble à genoux.
(Comprenez-vous?)

Où est-elle à cette heure?
Peut-être qu'elle pleure . . .
Où est-elle à cette heure?
Oh! du moins, soigne-toi, je t'en conjure!

O fraîcheur des bois le long de la route,
O châle de mélancolie, toute âme est un peu aux écoutes,
Que ma vie
Fait envie!
Cette impériale de diligence tient de la magie.

## VII
## SOLO BY MOONLIGHT

I smoke, stretched out facing the sky,
On the roof of a horse-drawn carriage,
My carcass is jolted, my soul
Dances like Ariel;
Not sweet nor bitter, my lovely soul dallies,
O roads, hillsides, O mists, O valleys,
My lovely soul, ah! let's recapitulate.

We loved each other crazily,
Without a word we let each other go;
Black moods were keeping me exiled,
Black moods which came from everything. So.

Her eyes said, "Do you understand?
Why don't you understand?"
But neither would take the first step;
We wanted to fall *together* to our knees.
(Do you understand?)

Where can she be at this hour?
Perhaps she weeps . . .
Where can she be at this hour?
Oh! take care of yourself, at least, for me!

O freshness of the woods along the way,
O shawl of melancholy, the soul's guard never quite goes away,
My life inspires
So many desires!
The roof of this carriage is magical today.

Accumulons l'irréparable!
Renchérissons sur notre sort!
Les étoiles sont plus nombreuses que le sable
Des mers où d'autres ont vu se baigner son corps;
Tout n'en va pas moins à la Mort.
Y a pas de port.

Des ans vont passer là-dessus,
On s'endurcira chacun pour soi,
Et bien souvent et déjà je m'y vois,
On se dira: "Si j'avais su . . . "
Mais mariés de même, ne se fût-on pas dit:
"Si j'avais su, si j'avais su! . . . "?
Ah! rendez-vous maudit!
Ah! mon cœur sans issue! . . .
Je me suis mal conduit.

Maniaques de bonheur,
Donc, que ferons-nous? Moi de mon âme,
Elle de sa faillible jeunesse?
O vieillissante pécheresse,
Oh! que de soirs je vais me rendre infâme
En ton honneur!

Ses yeux clignaient: "Comprenez-vous?
"Pourquoi ne comprenez-vous pas?"
Mais nul n'a fait le premier pas
Pour tomber ensemble à genoux. Ah! . . .

La Lune se lève,
O route en grand rêve! . . .

On a dépassé les filatures, les scieries,
Plus que les bornes kilométriques,
De petits nuages d'un rose de confiserie,

Let's accumulate the irreparable!
Treat ourselves worse than fate!
The stars are more numerous than the sand
Of seas where others have seen her body bathe;
But all to Death will report.
And there's no port.

Years will pass over all this,
We'll grow hard, each for himself,
And often and already I see myself
As we say to each other, "If I had only known . . ."
But even married, wouldn't we sometimes groan
"If I had known, if I had only known! . . ."?
Accursed rendevous!
Blind alley, that's my heart! . . .
I've behaved badly from the start.

Insane with happiness,
Thus, what shall we do? I with my soul,
She with her fallible youth?
O aging sinner,
Oh! so many evenings I'll be untrue
To myself, and vile, for you!

She winked at me, "Do you understand?
Why don't you understand?"
But neither took the first step
To fall to our knees together. Ah! . . .

Moonrise,
O road in dream surprised! . . .

We've passed spinning-mills and sawmills,
Nothing but milestones now;
Little clouds of confectioner's rose

Cependant qu'un fin croissant de lune se lève,
O route de rêve, ô nulle musique . . .
Dans ces bois de pins où depuis
Le commencement du monde
Il fait toujours nuit,
Que de chambres propres et profondes!
Oh! pour un soir d'enlèvement!
Et je les peuple et je m'y vois,
Et c'est un beau couple d'amants,
Qui gesticule hors la loi.

Et je passe et les abandonne,
Et me recouche face au ciel.
La route tourne, je suis Ariel,
Nul ne m'attend, je ne vais chez personne.
Je n'ai que l'amitié des chambres d'hôtel.

La lune se lève,
O route en grand rêve,
O route sans terme,
Voici le relais,
Où l'on allume les lanternes,
Où l'on boit un verre de lait,
Et fouette postillon,
Dans le chant des grillons,
Sous les étoiles de juillet.

O clair de Lune,
Noce de feux de Bengale noyant mon infortune,
Les ombres des peupliers sur la route . . .
Le gave qui s'écoute . . .
Qui s'écoute chanter . . .
Dans ces inondations du fleuve du Léthé . . .

Where a slender crescent of moon arose,
O dreaming road, O silent music . . .
In this pine wood which knows,
Since the world's beginning,
Only the night,
So many clean, deep bowers,
Oh! to elope for a night!
And I people them, and I see myself there,
And lovers, a handsome pair,
Gesticulate far from legal powers.

And I pass by and leave them,
And lie down facing the sky.
The road turns, I am Ariel,
No one waits for me, I'm going to no one's home.
I've only the frendship of hotel rooms.

The moon rises.
O road wrapped in dream,
O road without end,
Here is the inn
Where they light the lanterns,
Drink glasses of milk,
Then up postilion! and fly
To a singing of crickets
Under the stars of July.

O Moonlight,
Feast of Bengal fires drowning my misfortune,
Shadows of poplars along the road . . .
The little waterfall listens . . .
Listens to its own song . . .
In these floods of the river Lethe . . .

O Solo de lune,
Vous défiez ma plume.
Oh! cette nuit sur la route;
O Étoiles, vous êtes à faire peur,
Vous y êtes toutes! toutes!
O fugacité de cette heure . . .
Oh! qu'il y eût moyen
De m'en garder l'âme pour l'automne qui vient! . . .

Voici qu'il fait très, très frais,
Oh! si à la même heure,
Elle va de même le long des forêts,
Noyer son infortune
Dans les noces du clair de lune! . . .
(Elle aime tant errer tard!)
Elle aura oublié son foulard,
Elle va prendre mal, vu la beauté de l'heure!
Oh! soigne-toi, je t'en conjure!
Oh! je ne veux plus entendre cette toux!

Ah! que ne suis-je tombé à tes genoux!
Ah! que n'as-tu défailli à mes genoux!
J'eusse été le modèle des époux!
Comme le frou-frou de ta robe est le modèle des frou-frou.

O Solo by moonlight,
You defy me to write.
Oh! this night on the road;
You are frightening, Stars,
All of you! all!
O the flight of this night . . .
Oh! if only I might
Keep its soul for the coming fall! . . .

Now it's getting cold.
Oh! at this very moment, she
May be wandering the woods, like me,
To drown her misfortunes in moonlight feasts!
(She so likes staying out late!)
She'll have forgotten her scarf,
She'll get sick, the hour is so beautiful!
Oh! I beg you, take care of yourself!
Oh! no more of that coughing! Please!

Ah! why didn't I fall at your knees!
Ah! why didn't you faint at my knees!
I'd have been the perfect husband, for you!
As the frou-frou of your dress is the perfect frou-frou.

## VIII
## LEGENDE

Armorial d'anémie!
Psautier d'autumne!
Offertoire de tout mon ciboire de bonheur et de génie
A cette hostie si féminine,
Et si petite toux sèche maligne,
Qu'on voit aux jours déserts, en inconnue,
Sertie en de cendreuses toilettes qui sentent déjà l'hiver,
Se fuir le long des cris surhumains de la Mer.

Grandes amours, oh! qu'est-ce encor? . . .

En tous cas, des lèvres sans façon,
Des lèvres déflorées,
Et quoique mortes aux chansons,
Après encore à la curée,
Mais les yeux d'une âme qui s'est bel et bien cloîtrée.
Enfin, voici qu'elle m'honore de ses confidences.
J'en souffre plus qu'elle ne pense.

"Mais, chère perdue, comment votre esprit éclairé
"Et le stylet d'acier de vos yeux infaillibles,
"N'ont-ils su percer à jour la mise en frais
"De cet économique et passager bellâtre?"

    "Il vint le premier; j'étais seule près de l'âtre;
"Son cheval attaché à la grille
"Hénnissait en désespéré . . . "

    "C'est touchant (pauvre fille)
"Et puis après?"

# VIII
# LEGEND

Armorial of anemia!
Psalter of fall!
Offertory: my chalice full of happiness and genius
For that so feminine Host,,
And that dry little evil cough,
Passing anonymously through the emptiness of days,
Set into ash-grey as if winter weren't far off,
Fleeing herself the length of the Sea's superhuman cries.

True Love!—oh, not again!

In any case, those accommodating lips,
Lips whose bloom has gone,
Leaving them dead to song,
But avid still at the kill.
Behind her eyes her soul has taken the veil.
She grants me the privilege of hearing her tales of woe.
They distress me more than she will ever know.

"I wonder, dear lost one, how your enlightened mind,
And the steel stiletto of your infallible eyes,
Failed to see through the tawdry disguise
Of that cheap good-looking oaf who was passing by."

"He got there first. I was alone by the fire.
His horse, tied to the gate,
Neighed as if in despair . . . "

"How touching! (you poor child)
What happened then?"

"Oh! regardez là-bas, cet épilogue sous couleur de couchant!
"Et puis vrai,
"Remarquez que dès l'autumne, l'autumne!
"Les casinos,
"Qu'on abandonne
"Remisent leur piano;
"Hier l'orchestre attaqua
"Son dernier polka,
"Hier, la dernière fanfare
"Sanglotait vers les gares . . . "

(Oh! comme elle est maigre!
Que va-t-elle devenir?
Durcissez, durcissez,
Vous, caillots de souvenirs!)

—"Allons, les poteaux télégraphiques
"Dans les grisailles de l'exil
"Vous serviront de pleureuses de funérailles;
"Moi, c'est la saison qui veut que je m'en aille,
"Voici l'hiver qui vient.
"Ainsi soit-il.
"Ah! soignez-vous! Portez-vous bien.

"Assez! assez!
"C'est toi qui a commencé!

"Tais-toi! "Vos moindres clins d'yeux sont des parjures
"Laisse! avec vous autres rien ne dure.

"Va! je te l'assure,
"Si je t'aimais ce serait par gageure.

"Oh look! The epilogue is mascarading as sunset!
And don't forget,
As soon as it's autumn, autumn!
The casinos,
When no one comes,
Close their pianos;
The orchestra played
Its last polka yesterday,
The last fanfare left for the train
Sobbing all the way."

(Oh! She's thinner than ever!
What will become of her?
Grow hard, grow hard,
You clotted memories!)

"Come, come! the telegraph poles you pass,
Through exile's monotonous grey,
Will be useful at funerals—they weep for pay.
This season's too harsh for me, alas,
Winter is close, I can tell.
So be it.
Oh! Take care of yourself! Be well."

"That will do! That will do!
Who started all this if not you!"

"You blink an eye and I know you lie.
With your kind nothing has lasted yet!

Just give it up and go.
If I loved you, it would only be on a bet."

"Tais-toi! Tais-toi!
"Ou n'aime qu'une fois!"

"Ah! voici que l'on compte enfin avec Moi!

Ah! ce n'est plus l'autumne, alors
Ce n'est plus l'exil,
C'est la douceur des légendes, de l'âge d'or,
Des légendes des Antigones,
Douceur qui fait qu'on se demande:
"Quand donc cela se passait-il?"

C'est des légendes, c'est des gammes perlées,
Qu'on m'a tout enfant enseignées,
Oh! rien, vous dis-je, des estampes,
Les bêtes de la terre et les oiseaux du ciel
Enguirlandant les majuscules d'un Missel,
Il n'y a pas là de quoi saigner?

Saigner! moi pétri du plus pur limon de Cybèle!
Moi qui lui eusse été dans tout l'art des Adams
Des Edens aussi hyperboliquement fidèle
Que l'est le soleil chaque soir envers l'Occident! . . .

"Don't speak! don't speak!
Unless your love is unique."

At last you can see what is owed to Me!

Ah! If it's not autumn any more, then
Exile is at an end.
It's the sweetness of Golden Age legends,
Tales of the Antigones,
Sweetness that makes us wonder when
They were realities.

It's those legends, those legato scales
They taught me before I could read,
Oh! nothing at all, just pictures,
Beasts of the earth and birds of the sky
Enlivening capital letters of the Creed—
Wouldn't that make you bleed?

Bleed? When I'm made of Cybele's purest silt!
I who'd have been for her, with all the art of any Adam
Of Edens, as hyperbolically faithful
As the Sun is to the West every evening in its tilt! . . .

## IX

Oh! qu'une, d'Elle-même, un beau soir, sût venir
Ne voyant plus que boire à mes lèvres, ou mourir! . . .
Oh! Baptême!
Oh! baptême de ma Raison d'être!
Faire naître un "Je t'aime!"
Et qu'il vienne à travers les hommes et les dieux,
Sous ma fenêtre,
Baissant les yeux!
Qu'il vienne, comme à l'aimant la foudre,
Et dans mon ciel d'orage qui craque et qui s'ouvre,
Et alors, les averses lustrales jusqu'au matin,
Le grand clapissement des averses toute la nuit! Enfin
Qu'Elle vienne! et, baissant les yeux
Et s'essuyant les pieds
Au seuil de notre église, ô mes aïeux
Ministres de la Pitié,
Elle dise:
"Pour moi, tu n'es pas comme les autres hommes,
"Ils sont ces messieurs, toi tu viens des cieux.
"Ta bouche me fait baisser les yeux
"Et ton port me transporte
"Et je m'en découvre des trésors!
"Et je sais parfaitement que ma destinée se borne
"(Oh! j'y suis déjà bien habituée!)
"A te suivre jusqu'à ce que tu te retournes,
"Et alors t'exprimer comment tu es!
"Vraiment je ne songe pas au reste; j'attendrai
"Dans l'attendrissement de ma vie faite exprès.

# IX

Oh! if one of Them, some fine evening, would try—
Blind but to drink at my lips, or die! . . .
Oh! Baptized!
Oh! my whole life's Reason baptized!
Give birth to an "I love you!"
That would look at the gods and mankind,
And then, under my window,
Lower its eyes!
As lightning is drawn to keys,
May it crack and split open a stormy sky,
And then, until dawn, the lustral showers,
Showers like waves breaking all night long! And finally,
There she will be, lowering her eyes
And drying her feet
At the threshold of our church, O my ancestors,
Ministers of Compassion,
Let her repeat:
"For me you are not like the others,
They're only men, you, you come from Paradise.
Your mouth makes me lower my eyes,
And your gallant carriage carries me away
And I find treasures all along the way!
And I know perfectly well my destiny is bound
(Oh, I'm quite used to it already!)
To following you until you turn around,
And then to say how wonderful you are!
Truly, the rest means nothing to me; I'll just wait.
For the love of you my life was custom-made!

"Que je te dise seulement que depuis des nuits je pleure,
"Et que mes sœurs ont bien peur que je n'en meure.
"Je pleure dans les coins, je n'ai plus goût à rien;
"Oh! j'ai tant pleuré dimanche dans mon paroissien!

"Tu me demandes pourquoi toi et non un autre.
"Ah! laisse, c'est bien toi et non un autre.
"J'en suis sûre comme du vide insensé de mon cœur
"Et comme de votre air mortellement moqueur."
Ainsi, elle viendrait, évadée, demi-morte,
Se rouler sur le paillasson que j'ai mis à cet effet devant ma
porte.
Ainsi, elle viendrait à Moi avec des yeux absolument fous,
Et elle me suivrait avec ses yeux-là partout, partout!

But let me just tell you that all night long I cry,
And that my sisters are really afraid I'll die.
I sit in corners and weep. Nothing matters any more;
Oh! last Sunday in my prayerbook how I cried!
You ask me why it's you and no one else.
Ah! believe me, it's you and no one else.
I'm as sure as of my foolish heart's depression,
And your fatally mocking expression."
Thus she would come, escaped, half-dead, to my door
And roll on the mat I had just for that purpose put there.
Thus she would come to Me with absolutely mad eyes,
And follow me with those eyes everywhere, everywhere!

## X
## O GERANIUMS DIAPHANES

O géraniums diaphanes, guerroyeurs sortilèges;
Sacrilèges monomanes!
Emballages, dévergondages, douches! O pressoirs
Des vendanges des grands soirs!
Layettes aux abois,
Thyrses au fond des bois!
Transfusions, représailles,
Relevailles, compresses et l'éternelle potion,
Angelus! n'en pouvoir plus
De débacles nuptiales! de débacles nuptiales! . . .
Et puis, ô mes amours,
A moi, son tous les jours,
O ma petite mienne, ô ma quotidienne,
Dans mon petit intérieur,
C'est-à-dire plus jamais ailleurs!
O ma petite quotidienne!
Et quoi encore? Oh du génie,
Improvisons aux insomnies!
Et puis? L'observer dans le monde,
Et songer dans les coins:
"Oh, qu'elle est loin! Oh, qu'elle est belle!
"Oh, qui est elle? A qui est-elle?
"Oh, quelle inconnue! Oh, lui parler! Oh, l'emmener!"
(Et, en effet, à la fin du bal,
Elle me suivrait d'un air tout simplement fatal.)
Et puis, l'éviter des semaines
Après lui avoir fait de la peine,
Et lui donner des rendez-vous,
Et nous refaire un chez nous.
Et puis la perdre des mois et des mois,
A ne plus reconnaître sa voix! . . .

## X
## O DIAPHANOUS GERANIUMS

O diaphanous geraniums, warrior magic,
Monomaniacal blasphemy!
Delirium, debauchery, cold water! O a wine press
For those great evening harvests!
Layettes in distress
Bacchantes in the forests!
Transfusions, retaliations
Birth, church, compress and ever-alleviating
Angelus! can't bear these
Nuptial catastrophes! nuptial catastrophes! . . .
And then, O my loves,
For me, her day after day,
O my little my own, O my everyday,
In my own little place,
Meaning, never any place else again.
O my little everyday! . . .
What else? Oh, a bit of genius,
Insomniac improvisations!
And besides that? Watch her out in the world,
Stand around in corners making observations:
"Oh! She's so remote! Oh! How lovely!
Oh! who is she? Oh! whose is she?
A total stranger! If I could just speak to her! If we could elope!"
(And, in fact, at the end of the ball,
She would follow me, irresistibly enthralled!)
And then, not see her for weeks
After making her cry,
And say that we must meet
And give it another try.
Then lose her for months and rejoice
Not even to recognize her voice! . . .

Oui, le Temps salit tout,
Mais, hélas, sans en venir à bout.
Hélas! hélas! et plus la faculté d'errer,
Hypocondrie et pluie,
Et seul sous les vieux cieux,
De me faire le fou!
Le fou sans feux ni lieux
(Le pauvre, pauvre fou sans amours!)
Pour, alors, tomber bien bas
A me purifier la chair,
Et exulter au petit jour
En me fuyant en chemin de fer,
O Belles-Lettres. ô Beaux-Arts
Ainsi qu'un Ange à part!

J'aurai passé ma vie le long des quais
A faillir m'embarquer
Dans de bien funestes histoires,
Tout cela pour l'amour
De mon coeur fou de la gloire d'amour.
Oh, qu'ils sont pittoresques les trains manqués! . . .
Oh, qu'ils sont "à bientôt! à bientôt!"
Les bateaux
Du bout de la jetée! . . .
De le jetée bien charpentée
Contre la mer
Comme ma chair
Contre l'amour.

Time dirties everything—that's true,
But always has more to do.
Alas! alas! no heart for wandering,
Hypochondria and rain,
Alone under ancient skies
Driving myself insane!
A madman stripped of hearth and home,
(The poor, poor madman out of loves!)
And then to fall so low
That my flesh is purified,
And exult at the break of day,
Fleeing myself in a train,
O Literature! O Fine Art!
Like an Angel, set apart!

I'll have spent my life watching trains depart,
Never quite getting on board
For ill-omened affairs
Just because of the love in my heart
Mad for love in all its glory.
Oh, how picturesque are the trains we miss! . . .
How "See you soon! see you soon!"
Are boats
From the end of the jetty! . . .
The jetty standing so firmly
Against the sea
Like my body
Withstanding love.

## XI
## SUR UNE DÉFUNTE

Vous ne m'aimeriez pas, voyons,
Vous ne m'aimeriez pas plus,
Pas plus, entre nous,
Qu'une fraternelle Occasion? . . .
—-Ah! elle ne m'aime pas!
Ah! elle ne ferait pas le premier pas
Pour que nous tombions ensemble à genoux.
Si elle avait rencontré seulement
A, B, C ou D, au lieu de Moi,
Elle les eût aimés uniquement!
Je les vois, je les vois . . .
Attendez! Je la vois
Avec les nobles A, B, C ou D.
Elle était née pour chacun d'eux.
C'est lui, Lui, quel qu'il soit,
Elle le reflète;
D'un air parfait, elle secoue la tête
Et dit que rien, rien ne peut lui déraciner
Cette destinée.
C'est Lui; elle lui dit:
"Oh! tes yeux, ta démarche!
"Oh! le son fatal de ta voix!
"Voilà si longtemps que je te cherche!
"Oh! c'est bien Toi cette fois! . . . "
Il baisse un peu sa bonne lampe,
Il la ploie, Elle, vers son cœur,

## XI
## ABOUT A DEFUNCT LADY

Of course, you wouldn't love me;
You wouldn't love me—not more,
Not more, just between us,
Than a fraternal Opportunity? . . .
—Ah! she doesn't love me!
Ah! she wouldn't take the first step
So that we could fall together on our knees.
If she had only met
A, B, C or D, instead of Me,
She would have loved them exclusively!
I see them, I see them . . .
Wait! I see her
With the noble A, B, C or D.
She was born for every one of them.
It's he, He, whichever he is,
She mirrors;
How perfectly she shakes her head
And says that by nothing, nothing can she be led
Away from that destiny.
It's He; she tells him:
"Oh! your eyes, your walk!
Oh! irresistible, your talk!
I've been looking for you so long!
Oh! it's really You this time! . . ."
He lowers the lamp a little,
And bends her, Her, toward his heart,

Il la baise à la tempe
Et à la place de son orphelin cœur.
Il l'endort avec des caresses tristes,
Il l'apitoie avec de petites plaintes,
Il a des considérations fatalistes,
Il prend à témoin tout ce qui existe,
Et puis voici que l'heure tinte.
Pendant que je suis dehors
A errer avec elle au cœur,
A m'étonner peut-être
De l'obscurité de sa fenêtre.
Elle est chez lui, elle s'y sent chez elle.
Et, comme on vient de le voir,
Elle l'aime, éperdument fidèle,
Dans toute sa beauté des soirs! . . .
Je les ai vus! Oh! ce fut trop complet!
Elle avait l'air trop fidèle
Avec ses grands yeux tout en reflets
Dans sa figure toute nouvelle!
Et je ne serais qu'un pis-aller,
Et je ne serais qu'un pis-aller,
Comme l'est mon jour dans le Temps,
Comme l'est ma place dans l'Espace;
Et l'on ne voudrait pas que je m'accommodasse
De ce sort vraiment dégoûtant! . . .
Non, non! pour Elle, tout ou rien!
Et je m'en irai donc comme un fou,

He kisses her on her forehead
And on her orphan heart.
He puts her to sleep with sad caresses,
Awakens her pity with tales of woe,
Tells her their fate is in the stars,
On the cosmos itself takes his oath –
What happens after that you know.
Meanwhile, I wander apart
With her in my heart,
Being surprised, perhaps,
That her window is dark.
She is at his place; she feels at home,
.And, as we've just been seeing,
She loves him, obsessively faithful,
In all her beauty, like that of evenings . . .
I saw them! Oh! It was too complete!
She looked too true
With her large eyes all reflections
In her face so new!
And I would be second-rate,
And I would be second-rate,
Like my day in Time,
Like my place in Space;
Does anyone imagine I would deign to lower myself
To this truly disgusting fate!? . . .
No, no! For Her, all or nothing
And so I'll go crazily away

A travers l'automne qui vient,
Dans le grand vent où il y a tout!
Je me dirai: Oh! à cette heure,
Elle est bien loin, elle pleure,
Le grand vent se lamente aussi,
Et moi je suis seul dans ma demeure,
Avec mon noble cœur tout transi,
Et sans amour et sans personne,
Car tout est misère, tout est automne,
Tout est endurci et sans merci.
Et, si je t'avais aimée ainsi,
Tu l'aurais trouvée trop bien bonne! Merci!

Across the oncoming autumn,
Amid the great wind of everything!
I'll tell myself: Oh! at this hour,
She is far away, she weeps,
The great wind's weeping too.
And I am alone in my house
With my noble heart stone-cold,
And without love or anyone;
For all is misery, all is fall,
All has grown hard, there is no mercy.
You thought that I would play that game
For you? Thanks just the same!

## XII

Get thee to a nunnery: why wouldst thou be
a breeder of sinners? I am myself indifferent
honest; but yet I could accuse me of such
things, that it were better my mother had not
borne me. We are arrant knaves, all; believe
none of us. Go thy ways to a nunnery.

HAMLET

Noire bise, averse glapissante,
Et fleuve noir, et maisons closes,
Et quartiers sinistres comme des Morgues,
Et l'Attardé qui à la remorque traîne
Toute la misère du cœur et des choses,
Et la souillure des innocentes qui traînent,
Et crie à l'averse. "Oh? arrose, arrose
Mon cœur si brûlant, ma chair si intéressante!"
Oh! elle, mon cœur et ma chair, que fait-elle? . . .
Oh! si elle est dehors par ce vilain temps,
De quelles histoires trop humaines rentre-t-elle?
Et si elle est dedans,
A ne pas pouvoir dormir par ce grand vent,
Pense-t-elle au Bonheur,
Au bonheur à tout prix
Disant: tout plutôt que mon cœur reste ainsi incompris?
Soigne-toi, soigne-toi! pauvre cœur aux abois.
(Langueurs, débilité, palpitations, larmes,
Oh! cette misère de vouloir être notre femme!)
O pays, ô famille!
Et l'âme toute tournée

## XII

> Get thee to a nunnery: why wouldst thou be
> a breeder of sinners? I am myself indifferent
> honest; but yet I could accuse me of such
> things, that it were better my mother had not
> borne me. We are arrant knaves, all; believe
> none of us. Go thy ways to a nunnery.
>
> HAMLET

Black wind, downpour yelping,
Black river, and houses closed,
And neighborhoods sinister as Morgues,
And Someone who lingers dragging along
All the wrongs of the heart and of things
And the stains of innocents who drag along,
And cries to the storm: "Oh? then cool, refresh
My burning heart, my so interesting flesh!"
Oh! she, my heart and my flesh, where has she gone? . . .
Oh! If she's outside in this foul weather,
From what too human stories will she come in?
And if she's inside,
Unable to sleep in this great wind,
Does she think of Happiness,
Happiness at any price,
Saying: "Anything but let my heart stay so on ice!"
Take care of yourself, take care! poor hunted heart at bay.
(Languors, debility, palpitations, tears,
Oh! that wretchedness of wanting to be our wife!)
O country, O family!
And the soul quite turned away

D'héroïques destinées
Au delà des saintes vieilles filles,
Et pour cette année!
Nuit noire, maisons closes, grand vent,
Oh! dans un couvent, dans un couvent!
Un couvent dans ma ville natale
Douce de vingt mille âmes à peine,
Entre le lycée et la préfecture
Et vis-à-vis la cathédrale,
Avec ces anonymes en robes grises,
Dans la prière, le ménage, les travaux de couture;
Et que cela suffise . . .
Et méprise sans envie
Tout ce qui n'est pas cette vie de Vestale
Provinciale,
Et marche à jamais glacée,
Les yeux baissés.
Oh! je ne puis voir ta petite scène fatale à vif,
Et ton pauvre air dans ce huis-clos,
Et tes tristes petits gestes instinctifs,
Et peut-être incapable de sanglots!
Oh! ce ne fut pas et ce ne peut être,
Oh! tu n'es pas comme les autres,
Crispées aux rideaux de leur fenêtre
Devant le soleil couchant qui dans son sang se vautre!
Oh! tu n'as pas l'âge,
Oh! dis que tu n'auras jamais l'âge,
Oh! tu me promets de rester sage comme une image? . . .

From a heroic career
Beyond the saintly old maids,
And for this year!
Black night, storm, closed houses.
Oh! in a convent, in a convent!
A convent in my home town
Sweet with barely twenty thousand souls,
Between the high school and the court
And facing the cathedral,
With those anonymous ones in gray
Living to sew, to clean, or to pray,
And nothing more . . .
And, without envy, scorn
All that isn't this life of provincial
Vestals,
And walk forever frozen
With lowered eyes.
Oh! I can't bear to look at your destiny!
Your poor little face behind that locked door,
The sadness of your small reflexive gestures,
And perhaps you can't even cry anymore!
Oh! it wasn't and it can't be true,
Oh! you aren't like the others,
Clenched behind closed shutters,
Facing the setting sun which wallows in its blood!
Oh! you aren't old enough,
Oh! promise you'll never be old enough,
Oh! say that you'll always be good, as good as gold? . . .

La nuit est à jamais noire,
Le vent est grandement triste,
Tout dit la vieille histoire
Qu'il faut être deux au coin du feu,
Tout bâcle un hymne fataliste,
Mais toi, il ne faut pas que tu t'abandonnes
A ces vilains jeux! . . .
A ces grandes pitiés du mois de novembre!
Reste dans ta petite chambre,
Passe, à jamais glacée,
Tes beaux yeux irréconciliablement baissés.
Oh! qu'elle est là-bas, que la nuit est noire!
Que la vie est une étourdissante foire!
Que toutes sont créature, et que tout est routine!
Oh! que nous mourons!
Eh bien, pour aimer ce qu'il y a d'histoires
Derrière ces beaux yeux d'orpheline héroïne,
O Nature, donne-moi la force et le courage
De me croire en âge,
O Nature, relève-moi le front!
Puisque, tôt ou tard, nous mourrons . . .

The night is forever black,
The wind is grandly sad,
All tells the same old story
That we must be two at the fireside,
All blurts out a fatalistic hymn,
But you, you mustn't give in
To those nasty games! . . .
To those great November miseries!
Stay in your little room,
Pass by, forever frozen,
Irreconcilably lowered, your lovely eyes.
Oh! she is down there, and so black the night!
And life—what a dizzying fair!
How creature they are, and everything's trite!
Oh! and we are dying!
Oh well, to love what stories may lie
Behind the orphan heroine's beautiful eyes,
O Nature, give me courage and strength enough
To believe myself old enough,
O Nature, lift up my head!
Since sooner or later we'll be dead . . .

# PERSEUS AND ANDROMEDA
## or the Happiest of the Three

# Perseus and Andromeda,

## or

## The Happiest of the Three

### I

OH, MONOTONOUS AND UNDESERVED HOMELAND! . . .

The island all alone, duned yellow gray; under migratory skies; and everywhere the impasse of the sea, imposing a limit on views, cries, hope and melancholy.

The sea! From whatever side observed, hour after hour, at whatever moment glimpsed: always itself, never remiss, always alone, empire of the antisocial, vast mute history, unassimilable cataclysm;—as if the liquid state we see it in were only a lapse! And the days when it starts to agitate this (liquid) state! And those, even more intolerable, when it takes on the wounded metallic look of a face which has nothing resembling itself to look at, which has no one. The sea, always the sea without a moment's respite! In short, not promising material for a friendship (oh, please! give up that idea, and even the hope of sharing the ill will that follows confidences, no matter how long you two have been together).

Oh monotonous and undeserved homeland! . . . But when will all this come to an end?—Well, concerning the infinite: space monopolized by the sea alone, indifferently limitless, time expressed by skies alone, crisscrossed indifferently by seasons of migratory birds, gray, screeching, and untameable!—What are we to make of this, what can we do with so much murky and ineffable sulking? Warmhearted from the outset, we might just as well die right now.

The sea, this afternoon, is nothing special—deep green as far as the eye can reach; the froth as far as the eye can reach of countless whitecaps igniting, fizzling out, rekindling, like a flock of countless sheep who swim, and drown, and reappear, and never arrive, and will let night catch up with them. And above it all, the frolicking of the four winds, frolicking for the love of it, for the pleasure of wasting this afternoon whipping up the crests of foam into iridescent dust. Oh! when a ray of sunlight passes over the backs of waves it's the caress of a rainbow like a shimmering dolphin who surfaces and at once submerges, stupidly mistrustful.

And that's all; oh, undeserved and monotonous homeland! . . . Deep into the little cove, its two caves feathered with eiderdown and pale kelp, comes the vast and monotonous sea, panting and streaming. But its complaint does not drown out the little moans, the little high-pitched hoarse moans of Andromeda, who lies there on her stomach, chin in hand, and faces the horizon, vacantly scrutinizing the mechanism of the waves, the waves being born then dying out, as far as the eye can reach. Andromeda bemoans her fate. She moans, but suddenly it occurs to her that her lament is harmonizing with those of the sea and the wind, two antisocial beings, two powerful cronies who don't even notice her. She stops abruptly, and looks around for someone to blame. She calls out:

—Monster! . . .

—Kitten? . . .

—Hey! Monster! . . .

—Kitten? . . .

—What are you doing over there?

The Dragon-Monster, crouched at the entrance to his cave, his hindquarters half underwater, turns around, his spine shimmering with all the jewels of the deep sea Golcondas, compassionately raises his eyelids fringed with multicolored cartilaginous macramé, displays two great watery sea-green pupils, and says (in the voice of a distinguished gentleman who has seen better days):

—As you can tell, Kitten, I am breaking and polishing pebbles for your slingshot; more birds will be flying by before sunset.

—Stop it, the noise hurts my ears. And I don't want to kill any more birds. Why not let them pass, let them go home.—Oh migrations that don't see me as they pass, oh hordes of waves that come to die here, bringing me nothing, I'm so bored! Ah, I'm really sick this time! . . . —Monster? . . .

—Kitten?

—Why don't you bring me jewels anymore? What have I done, uncle? Tell me!

The Monster shrugs his shoulders sumptuously, scratches in the sand to his right, lifts up a large smooth pebble, and takes out a fistful of rosy pearls and crystallized anemones he's been saving for just such a moment. He sets them down beneath Andromeda's pretty nose. Still lying on her stomach, chin in hand, Andromeda sighs without moving:

—And what if I refuse them coldly, inexplicably?

The Monster snatches back his treasure and sends it down to the native underwater Golcondas.

Then Andromeda rolls in the sand and moans, pulling her hair in pathetic disorder over her face:

—Oh, my rosy pearls, my crystallized anemones! Oh, this will be the death of me, the death of me! And it will be all your fault. Ah, you know nothing about the Irreparable!

But she calms down immediately and comes crawling over to stretch out, cuddly as usual, beneath the Monster's chin, encircling his neck, that viscously purplish-blue neck, with her white arms. The Monster sumptuously shrugs his shoulders and, with his usual kindness, starts secreting wild musk from every place he feels the touch of those firm slender arms, the slender arms of the dear child, who soon sighs again:

—Oh Monster, oh Dragon, you say you love me, and you're no help at all. You see how I'm perishing of boredom and you're no help. How I'd love you if you could cure me, if there was something you could do! . . .

—Oh noble Andromeda, Princess of Ethiopia! This Dragon-in-spite-of-himself, this poor monster can only answer you with a vicious circle: when you love me I will cure you, for you will cure me when you love me.

—The same old oracular riddle! But I've told you: I like you a lot!

—I know that as well as you do. Let's drop it; I'm still just a poor monster of a dragon, an unfortunate Catoblepas.

—If you'd only take me on your back and carry me to places where there are people. (Ah, I would so like to launch myself into society!) Once there, I will absolutely give you a real little kiss for your trouble.

—I've already told you it's impossible. Here is where our destinies must unfold.

—Oh, tell me what that means! Tell me everything!

—I don't know any more than you, oh noble red-headed Andromeda.

—Our destinies! Our destinies! But I'm getting older every day! It can't go on like this!

—Want to go for a little swim?

—You and your little swims. Can't you think up something new?

Andromeda throws herself flat on her belly, digging and scratching at the sand the length of her legitimately hungry thighs, and then her little moans begin again, her hoarse high-pitched moans. The monster thinks it the right moment to imitate the breaking falsetto of this poor child, mocking her romantic grievances, so he begins in a neutral tone:

—Pyramus and Thisby. Once upon a time . . .

—No, no! No dead stories or I'll kill myself!

—Come on now, that's enough. Snap out of it! Go fishing, go hunting, write poems, play the conch north, south, east and west, work on your shell collection. Or—I have it!—carve symbols all over the most recalcitrant rocks (that's what makes time go by!) . . .

—I can't, I can't. I'm telling you, I've lost my taste for everything.

—Wait, look! Kitten, look up—oh! Do you want your slingshot? It's the autumn migration's third flock since this morning. Their triangle is flying past in its even palpitation, without stragglers. They are passing by, and that evening they will be so faraway . . .

—Oh, if only I could go where they're going! If only I could love! . . . cries poor Andromeda.

The little one jumps up, crazed, and with intermittent howls and galloping leaps, she disappears across the gray dunes of the island.

The Monster smiles good-naturedly and returns to polishing his pebbles. Just so must the wise Spinoza have polished his eyeglass lenses.

## II

LIKE A LITTLE WOUNDED ANIMAL, ANDROMEDA GALLOPS, GALLOPS WITH the spindly gait of the wading bird in a landscape dotted with ponds, further maddened by having ceaselessly to fling aside her long red hair, which the wind pastes across her eyes and mouth. Where is she going thus, oh puberty, puberty! through the wind and the dunes, baying as do the wounded?

Andromeda! Andromeda!

Her perfect feet in espadrilles of lichen, a necklace of raw coral threaded on a strand of algae at her neck, impeccably naked, naked and inflexible, this is the way she grew up, out of doors, galloping, swimming through squalls, sunlight. Her face and hands are no more nor less white than the rest of her body; her whole small person, with its silky red mane tumbling to her knees, is all the same shade of washed terra cotta. (Oh, those bounding leaps!) All bone and sinew, all suntanned, this pubescent wild child, with her oddly long fine legs, her proud straight hips, tapering toward her breasts, two childish hints of breasts, so inadequate that when she gallops her breathing scarcely lifts them at all (and when and how could they have grown, always pushing against the wind, the salty wind of the open sea, and against the furiously glacial showers of the waves?) and her long neck, and her head small as a baby's, completely wild, framed in its auburn fleece, her eyes sometimes as piercing as the eyes of sea birds, sometimes as dull as the waters of everyday. In short, the ideal young lady. Oh, those bounding leaps! and the wailing of a young girl wounded by a hard life! As I say, she grew up like this, out of doors, naked and inflexible, suntanned, with her red mane, galloping, swimming through squalls, sunlight. But where could she be going, oh puberty, puberty?

Way at the end, on a promontory, an odd cliff; Andromeda climbs a labyrinth of natural ramps. From the narrow platform on top she looks out over the island and the undulating solitude that isolates the island. In the middle of this platform the rains have dug a basin, which Andromeda has lined with pebbles of black ivory and filled with clear water. And ever since one spring, this has been her mirror, and her only secret in the world.

For the third time today she comes to look at her reflection. She does not smile, she sulks, she tries to plumb the solemnity of her eyes, but they do not give up their depth. And her mouth! She never tires of adoring the innocent blossom of her mouth. Oh, who will ever understand her mouth?

—I do look mysterious! she thinks dreamily.

Then she tries sophisticated poses.

—Anyway, that's me, no more, no less; take it or leave it.

Then she thinks how undistinguished she is, really.

But she comes back to her eyes. Ah! her eyes are beautiful, touching, and all hers. She never tires of making their acquaintance. She could stay there, questioning them, until the last glimmers of day. Ah! why do they insist on looking like that, so infinite? Why isn't she someone else, so she could spend her life gazing at them, dreaming of their secret, silently! . . .

She stares at herself, to no avail! Her face, just like her, is still waiting, serious and distant.

So she turns to her red mane, she tries out twenty different hairdos; in the end they're all too cumbersome for her small head.

And here come rain clouds to disrupt her mirror. Beneath a stone, there is a dried fish skin that serves as her nail file. She sits and does her nails. The clouds arrive, the clouds burst in a great rumbling downpour. Andromeda tumbles down the cliff and starts galloping back toward the sea and whimpers into the downpour:

Ah! If anyone knew
What to do
For Andromeda's boo-boo!
Boo hoo! Boo-boo!
Tears stream down her childish breast, so sad is this song. And the storm
is already faraway, and gusts of wind ruffle her hair . . .
Boo hoo!
Since there's no help for me,
I'll throw myself into the sea!
Boo hoo!

But it's a swim she's running to take, a simple swim. Although just as
she's about to dive in, she swerves. Swimming, nothing but swimming!
She's so tired of playing with her coarsely dumpy sisters the waves—she's
had more than enough of their skin and manners. So she stretches out on
her back in the drenched sand, her arms open in a cross, her head toward
the incoming breakers. It's better this way, she has only to wait for a good
wallop of water. After a threatening to-and-fro, a rearing coil rushes up and
leaps on her. Eyes closed, Andromeda takes it, unflinching, with the long
sob of a sacrificial victim, and wraps herself around this rushing ice-cold
pillow, which flows off, and leaves nothing in her arms . . .

Dazed, she sits up, looks at her pitiful streaming flesh, picks from her
hair the strands of algae the shower has braided into it. Then, resolutely,
she throws herself into the water. She beats the waves like a windmill, dives,
surfaces, breathes, floats on her back. A new broadside of waves arrives,
and Andromeda, crazed, is knocked over, but leaps up like a carp, trying
to straddle the crests! She captures one by its mane and rides it an instant,
with cruel cries; a second traitorously rushes over to unseat her, but she
grabs another. And then they all shy away beneath her, unwilling to wait
around. But the sea takes to the game and grows unruly, so Andromeda
floats, washes up dishevelled on the beach. She crawls beyond the reach of
the waves, and stays there, sunk into the moving sands, flat on her stomach.

And now a new sheet of showers passes over the island. Andromeda does not move, but moaning under the great diluvian rumble, she welcomes the rain, the yelping rain, which playfully blows bubbles in the ravine of her back. She feels the sodden sand yield little by little beneath her, and she twists to sink into it deeper. (Oh! let me be submerged, let me be buried alive!)

But the storm clouds depart just as they came, the rumbling becomes indistinct, she's left with the Atlantic solitude of the island. Andromeda sits and looks at the horizon, the horizon which clears, nothing interesting about it. What to do? When the wind has wiped her poor self dry, she runs, a little exhausted, to climb back up her promontory, where at least someone intelligent, her mirror, is waiting for her.

The nasty rain has sullied her sad mirror's purity.

Andromeda turns away, she is about to burst out sobbing, but here comes a huge sea bird, aiming, all sails set, as though straight for the island, for the cliff, for her perhaps! She utters a long whimper of appeal, sinks down against the rock, her arms extended in a cross, and closes her eyes. Oh, if only the bird would dive at her little Promethean self, exposed here by the gods! If only it would perch on her knees and with an implacably beneficial beak begin to peck away the burning nucleus of her boo-boo.

But she feels the flight of the great bird passing; she opens her eyes, he is already faraway, preoccupied, no doubt, with far more interesting corpses.

Poor Andromeda, clearly she wants to exorcise her existence, but which end to take hold of first?

What to do? Why not reconsider the sea, so limited and yet so uniquely open to hope . . . Then too, how little-girlish is her torment in the face of so much solitude as far as the eye can reach! With just one wave the sea can fill her to the very brim; but she, small slender bit of flesh, how could she soothe and warm up the sea? Ah, in vain would she stretch out her arms! . . . And anyway, how weary she is! In the past she galloped around her domain all day long; now, her heart beats too fast . . . Another of those great sea birds is passing by. If only she could adopt one, cradle it! They never stop off at the island. You have to kill them with slingshots to look at them up close.

To cradle, to be cradled, the sea does not willingly cradle.

The wind has fallen, there's a temporary lull as the horizon wipes the melancholy slate clean for the ceremony of sunset.

To cradle, to be cradled! . . . Andromeda's weary little head fills with maternal cadences and there comes back to her the only human lullaby she knows, the legend of The Truth With Regard to Everything, a little sacred text her guardian the Dragon sang over her childhood cradle:

"In the beginning was Love, the universal organizing principle, unconscious, infallible. Immanent in the interdependent vortices of phenomena, it is the infinite aspiration toward the Ideal.

"For the Earth, the Sun is its keystone, the Reservoir, the Spring.

"This is why morning and springtime are happiness, twilight and autumn death. (But since nothing is more thrilling to superior organisms than to feel themselves dying, knowing that they aren't, twilight and autumn, the drama of the sun and of death, are quintessentially aesthetic.)

"The impulse toward the Ideal established once and for all, and once and for all, in infinite space, is manifest in innumerable worlds that form, go through their organic evolution as far as their elements permit, and then disintegrate to make way for the blossoming of new laboratories.

"As for the initial unconscious, it has only to occupy itself with rising higher, it has its own work to do, which it supervises in several livelier and more significant worlds; nothing could distract it from its dream of tomorrow.

"And as for those planets which, having run through the evolution already known to the Unconscious, lack sufficient depth to be of service as a laboratory for the Being of tomorrow—as for them, the Unconscious simply ignores them; their little evolutions continue doggedly, as a result of the initial impulse, like so many identical experimental trials of an old and far too well-known banality.

"And thus, just as the evolution of the human fetus inside its mother's womb is a reflection in miniature of all earthly evolution, so too earthly evolution is but a reflection of the Great Unconcious Evolution in Time.

"Elsewhere, elsewhere in infinite space, the Unconscious is more advanced! What celebrations! . . .

"The Earth, even if it should yield beings superior to Man, is no more than a repeated, unimportant experiment in apprenticeship.

"But the good Earth, descended from the Sun, is everything to us because we possess five senses and the whole earth speaks to them. Oh, succulences, marvelous plasticity, fragrances, sounds, astonishments as far as the eye can see, Love! Oh life of mine!

"Man is no more than an insect beneath the heavens; but let him respect himself and he becomes God. One spasm of a being is worth the whole of nature."

Thus Andromeda drones on gloomily, faced with yet another nightfall, deriving from her recitation only the sweetness of a lesson learned by heart. Ah! she stretches and moans.

Ah! how long will she stretch and moan? . . .

And she says, loud and clear, to the Atlantic solitude of her island:

—Yes, but suppose some I-don't-know-what sixth sense is yearning to unfold, and nothing, nothing calls it forth! Ah! The point is I'm all by myself, and very much on my own, and I don't know how it's all going to end.

She caresses her arms, and then, exasperated, gnashes her teeth, claws at herself, then carefully cuts herself with a flint shard found nearby.

—But, oh gods, I can't take my own life, just to see what happens! . . .

She's crying.

—No, no! They've left me here much too long! It's pointless to come for me now, to take me away. I'll bear a grudge my whole life long, I'll always a little grudge.

# III

YET ANOTHER EVENING FALLS, ANOTHER SUNSET IS ABOUT TO STRUT LIKE a dandy—classic! More than classic! Andromeda flings back her red mane and retraces her steps home.

The monster does not come to meet her. How come? The monster isn't there anymore! She calls:

—Monster! Monster! . . .

No response. She sounds the conch. Nothing. She returns to the cliff that overlooks the island, and sounds the conch, and calls. My God! . . . No one. She goes home.

—Monster! Monster! . . . Disaster! What if he has dived underwater to stay, what if he's gone, leaving me alone, on the pretext that I tormented him too much, I made his life miserable!

Oh! The island at nightfall appears to her impossibly, extraordinarily lost! She throws herself on the sand in front of her cave, and moans lengthily, moans that she wants to let herself die, that she should have known . . .

When she gets up, the monster is there in his customary mud, busy piercing holes in one of those conches out of which he makes her ocarinas.

—Well, there you are, she says. I thought you'd left.

—Hardly. As long as I live I will be your jailer without fear and without reproach.

—What did you say?

—I said that as long as I live . . .

—Right, right; we know.

Silence and horizon, the horizon of the seas swept clean for the sunset.

—What if we played checkers? sighs Adromeda, visibly on edge.

—Let's play checkers. The cave's threshold is inlaid with a checkerboard made of black and white mosaic. But scarcely has the game begun wh[en] Andromeda, visibly on edge, jostles the pieces.

—It's no use, I'd lose—I can't concentrate. It's not my fault, [I'm] on edge.

Silence and horizon! After all the afternoon's excitement, the air is becalmed and spends some moments in silence before the classic retreat of the Star.

The Star! . . .
On the glistening horizon, sirens are holding their breath,
The sunset's scaffoldings are rising;
From beacon to beacon, the tiered theatrical masonry builds up;
Fireworks experts add the finishing touches;
A series of gold moons is blossoming, like the open mouths of trumpets drawn up into ranks, hosts of annunciatory heralds fulminating!
The slaughterhouse is ready, the hanging tapestries are reefed;
On palanquins of diadems, and harvests of Venitian lanterns, and sparkles and sprays of light,
Held in by dams of false gold, pillaged already,
The Pasha Star,
His Red Eminence,
His robes shattering,
Descends, mortally triumphal,
Minute after minute, through the Sublime Gate! . . .
And lies on his side, exhausted, marbled with cantankerous stigmata.
Quick, somebody nudge this punctured pumpkin with your foot, and then—
Farewell baskets, the harvest's in! . . .
Ranked trumpets are lowered, ramparts crumble, their beacons like prismatic carafes! Cymbals fly, courtisans stumble among the flags, tents are folded, the army breaks camp in panic, carrying off Western basilisks, winepresses, idols, bundles, vestal virgins, desks, ambulances, band platforms, all the official paraphernalia.
And they fade into a fine cloud of pink gold.
In a word, everything went marvelously well! . . .

lous, fabulous! drools the Taciturn Monster ecstatically, his great
till lit with the last glints from the West.

—Farewell baskets, the harvest's in! sighs Andromeda duskily, her red mane looking meager after all those flames.

No more to do than light the evening fire, eat supper, and bless the moon before going to bed, to wake up tomorrow and begin a day just like today.

Silence and horizon are ready for the mortuary Moon, when—oh, blessèd be the gods who send, precisely at this moment! a third character.

He arrives like a rocket, our sparkling hero, on a snowy Pegasus whose wings, tinted with sunset, are atremble, clearly reflected in the immense melancholy mirror of the Atlantic on a beautiful evening! . . .

No doubt about it: Perseus!

Her girlish heart beating so fast she can scarcely breathe, Andromeda runs to snuggle beneath the Monster's chin.

And great tears spring to the Monster's eyelashes like the girandoles on balustrades. He speaks in a voice we've never heard from him before:

—Andromeda, oh noble Andromeda, don't worry, it's Perseus. It's Perseus, son of Danae from Argos and of Jupiter changed into a shower of gold. He's going to kill me and take you with him.

—Of course he won't, he won't kill you!

—He will kill me.

—He won't kill you if he loves me.

—He can only take you with him by killing me.

—No, we'll work it out. Things always work out. Leave it to me.

Andromeda has stood up from her usual place and is staring.

—Andromeda, Andromeda! Think of the value of your unique flesh, the value of your fresh soul—a misalliance can be entered into so fast!

But does she hear? Face thrust forward, elbows out, fingers clenched at her hips, she stands on the shore, altogether brave and feminine.

Miraculous and brimming with chic, Perseus approaches; the wings of his hippogriff beat more slowly; and the closer he gets, the more provincial Andromeda feels herself to be, and doesn't know what to do with her charming arms.

Within a few meters of Andromeda, the hippogriff, elegantly trained, stops and kneels just above the waves, holding himself aloft in a pink quivering of wings, and Perseus bows. Andromeda lowers her head. So here is her fiancé. What will his voice sound like, and what will he say first?

But he's off again without a word, backs away, rushes forward and begins to fly in ovals, passing again and again in front of her, gamboling just above the miraculous mirror of the sea, narrowing his orbit more and more toward Andromeda, as though to give this little virgin time to admire him and desire him. An extraordinary spectacle, that's the truth! . . .

This time, smiling at her, he has passed so close she could have touched him!

Perseus rides side-saddle, coquettishly crossing his feet in their fine linen sandals; from the pommel of his saddle hangs a mirror; he is beardless, his pink and smiling mouth looks, we might say, like a pomegranite cut open; his hollow chest is lacquered with a rose, on his arms are tattoos of hearts pierced by an arrow, he has lilies painted on the fleshy part of his calves, he wears an emerald monocle, and numerous rings and bracelets; from his gilded baldric hangs a little pearl-handled sword.

On his head Perseus wears Pluto's helmet, which confers invisibility; he has the wings and winged sandals of Mercury, and Minerva's divine shield; bobbing at his belt is the head of the Gorgon Medusa, the mere sight of which changed giant Atlas into a mountain, as we all know; and his hippogriff is that very Pegasus Bellerophon was riding when he killed the Chimera. Our young hero looks remarkably sure he can't lose.

Our young hero stops his hippogriff in front of Andromeda and, as the open pomegranate of his mouth goes on smiling, he starts to twirl his adamantine sword. Andromeda doesn't move, ready to weep with uncertainty, seeming to wait only for the sound of this character's voice before abandoning herself to her fate.

Off to the side, the Monster holds his tongue.

Gracefully, Perseus turns his mount, who, without disturbing the mirror of the water, kneels before Andromeda, his side to her; the young knight joins his hands to make a stirrup and, tilting them in front of the young captive, says in a hopelessly artificial throaty voice:

—Upsadaisy! Off to Cythera! . . .

Oh, why not get it over with! As Andromeda starts to place her uncouth foot in the delicate stirrup, she turns toward the Monster in sign of fare-well. Not so fast! The latter has just plunged between them, underneath the hippogriff, and reappears rearing, his two feet firmly planted, to expose the purplish-blue cavern of his mouth which shoots out a lance of flame! The hippogriff is alarmed, Perseus moves back to get some room, and starts blustering at the top of his lungs. The Monster waits for him. Perseus hurls himself forward, but instantly stops:

—Ah! You won't have the satisfaction of my killing you in front of her, he cries. Luckily, thanks to the just gods I have more than one string to my bow. I am going to . . . Medusify you!

The gods' little darling unhooks the Gorgon's head from his belt. Sawed off at the neck, the celebrated head is alive, but alive with stagnant and empoisoned life, all black from apoplexy repressed, her white and blood-shot eyes in a rigid stare, and rigid, too, the rictus of decapitation, nothing about her moving except her viper hair.

Perseus takes hold of her by that hair, whose blue gold-speckled coils make him new bracelets, and thrusts her at the Dragon, shouting to Andromeda: "You, lower your eyes!"

But miraculously the spell doesn't work!

The spell will not work!

In fact, with an incredible effort, the Gorgon has closed her petrifying eyes.

The good Gorgon has recognized our Monster. She remembers the rich breeze-filled days when she and her two sisters lived next-door to this Dragon, at that time the guardian of the garden of the Hesperides, the mar-velous garden of the Hesperides situated near the Columns of Hercules. No, no, a thousand times no, she will not petrify her old friend!

Perseus is still waiting, his arm extended, aware of nothing. The contrast is a little too grotesque between his brave and magisterial gesture and the fact it's such a dud, and our untamed little Andromeda can't hold back a certain smile, a certain smile that Perseus intercepts! The hero is astonished, what's the matter with his good Medusa's head? And although his helmet basically makes him invisible, it isn't without trepidation that he risks looking at the Gorgon's face, to see what's happening there. It's very simple, the petrifying spell didn't work because the Gorgon has closed her eyes.

Furious, Perseus hooks the head back on his belt, brandishes his sword with a conquering snigger, and clasping Minerva's divine shield to his heart, he spurs his mount (oh, just as the full moon rises in the distance over the miraculous Atlantic mirror!) and swoops down on the Dragon, poor wingless heap. Perseus circles him with dazzling gymnastics, he sticks him to the left, he pricks him to the right, and at last drives him back into a crevice, where he sinks his sword so marvelously through the middle of his forehead that the poor Dragon collapses and, with his dying breath, has only time to moan:

—Farewell, noble Andromeda. I loved you, and we could have had a future, if you'd wanted it. Farewell, you'll often think of this.

The Monster is dead. But Perseus is over-excited, despite the inevitability of his triumph, and he has to savage the deceased! and slash him repeatedly! and put out his eyes! and make mincemeat of him! Until finally Andromeda calls a halt.

—Enough, enough! You can see he's dead.

Perseus replaces his sword in his baldric, pats his blond curls into place, takes a throat lozenge, and descending from his mount, whose neck he strokes:

—And now, my lovely! says he in a syrupy voice.

Andromeda, still there, irreproachable and inflexibly naked, with her black seagull eyes, asks:

—Do you love me, do you really love me?

—Love you? But I adore you, of course! Life without you would be unbearable and full of shadows! Love you? Why just look at yourself! And he extends his mirror to her. But in what seems a paroxysm of surprise, Andromeda gently pushes this item away. He pays no attention, and hastens to add:

—Ah, of course! We must have a little decoration!

He takes off one of his necklaces, a necklace of gold coins (a souvenir of his mother's wedding) and tries to place it around her neck. She gently pushes it away, but he takes advantage of her gesture to put his two hands around her waist.

The little wounded animal wakes up! Andromeda cries out, the cry of gulls on the worst days, a cry that echoes across the island, already completely dark:

—Don't touch me! Oh, forgive me, forgive me, but to tell the truth, all this has happened so fast! I beg of you, let me wander around a little, leave me alone to say a last farewell . . .

She turns with a gesture of embrace toward the island and her dear cliff, where the night is falling, the reliable night, oh! forever reliable! so reliable and intangible that Andromeda immediately turns away from it toward the one who is to tear her out of her past, at the risk of all she has. And she catches him unawares: he is yawning! An elegant yawn that he attempts to make into an open-pomegranate smile.

Oh, night on the island of the past! Monster killed so unvaliantly, Monster without a tomb! Excessively elegant lands of tomorrow . . . Andromeda can only cry out:

—Go! Go! You disgust me! I'd rather die alone. Go! you've come to the wrong address.

—Well, really! That's a fine way to talk! Listen, little girl, people like me don't wait to be told twice. And I can't say much for your complexion either.

He twirls his adamantine sword, climbs back in the saddle, and shoots off, without a backward glance, into the spell cast by the rising moon; you can hear him yodel; he shoots off like a meteor, he fades out toward elegant and undemanding lands . . .

Oh, night on the poor everyday island! . . . What a dream! . . .

Andromeda remains there, head down, numb, in front of the horizon, the magical horizon that she rejected, that she could not but reject, oh gods who gave her such a heart!

She goes to the Monster, still lying in his corner, inanimate, flaccid and purple, poor, poor Monster. What a waste! . . .

As in the good old days, she comes to stretch out underneath his chin, now dead—she has to lift it up—, and wraps her little arms around his neck. He is still warm. Curious, she lifts an eyelid with her index finger. The lid uncovers a gouged-out eye, then falls back. She pushes aside the locks of his mane and counts the bloody holes made by the nasty diamond sword. And past and future tears, silent tears flow from her eyes.

How beautiful life was, with him on this island! And unconsciously stroking his eyelashes, she remembers. She remembers what he was to her, a good friend, an accomplished gentleman, an industrious scholar, an eloquent poet. And her little heart bursts into sobs, and she doubles up beneath the inert chin of the unappreciated Monster, and clasps him by the neck, and, too late, implores him:

—Oh, poor poor Monster! Why didn't you tell me everything before! Then you wouldn't be here, killed by that nasty Comic Opera hero. And me, all alone in the night! We would still have lovely days. You should have seen that I was only going through a phase, with all that moodiness, and that fatal curiosity. Oh, triple-catastrophic curiosity! I have killed my friend, I've killed my only friend! My nurturing father, my tutor. No point now in making these callous shores resound with laments! Noble Monster, his last words were for me: "Farewell Andromeda, I loved you and we could have had a future, if you'd wanted it!"—Oh, now at last I understand the depth of your great soul! And your silences, and your afternoons, and everything! Too late, too late! But doubtless that was what the gods ordained. Oh, just gods, take half of Andromeda's life, take half of my life and give me back his, so that I can love and serve him from now on with loyalty and kindness. Oh gods, do this for me, you who read my heart and know how much

I really loved him, even blinded by my adolescent whims, and loved only him, and will love him forever!

And noble Andromeda grazes the closed eyelids of the Dragon with the adorable blossom of her mouth. And suddenly draws back! . . . For at these fateful words, these redemptive kisses, the Monster gives a start, opens his eyes, weeps silently, and looks at her . . . And then he speaks:

—Noble Andromeda, thank you. The period of adversity is over. I am being reborn, and I'll be reborn fit to love you as you should be loved, and may there be no word nor minute to give a name to your happiness. But now let me tell you who I am and what my fate was. I came of the accursed race of Cadmus, dedicated to the Furies! In the groves of Arcadia, I taught people to deride existence and worship nothingness. To punish me, the gods of life made me a Dragon, condemning me to guard the treasures of the earth, until the very moment when a virgin loved me—me, a monster, for myself. First, as a dragon with three heads, I spent ages guarding the golden apples in the garden of the Hesperides; Hercules arrived and slit my throat. Then I passed into Colchis, where Phryxus of Thebes was to arrive with his sister Helle, on the ram with the golden fleece. An oracle had led me to believe that Helle would be the promised virgin. But she drowned on the trip and gave her name to the straits of the Hellespont. (I've since found out she wasn't very pretty.) Then along came those strange Argonauts, the likes of which will not be seen again! . . . Splendid times! Jason was at their head, Hercules followed, and his friend Theseus, and Orpheus who tried to charm me with his lyre (and who later came to such a tragic end!) and also the Twins, Castor, tamer of horses, and Pollux, capable boxer. Times gone by! . . .

Oh, their bivouacs, and the fires they lit in the evening! But at last I got my throat slit, in front of the Golden Fleece of the Holy Grail, thanks to the potions of Medea, burning with mad love for the sumptuous Jason. And the cycle began again; I knew Eteocles and Polyneices, and pious Antigone, and the perfecting of weapons that put an end to heroic times. And finally the strange and oppressive Ethiopia, and your father, and you, oh noble Andromeda, Andromeda more beautiful than all others, to whom I owe the power to make you so happy that there will be neither word nor minute for you to give a name to your happiness.

At the end of this amazing speech, the Dragon—without a word of warning!—is changed into a perfect young man. Leaning on his elbow at the entrance to the cave, his human skin flooded with the charms of moonlight, he talks about the future. Andromeda does not dare acknowledge him and turns away a little, smiling into the void, swept by those feelings of sadness that visit her from time to time, when she's about to do something rash (for her soul has always been easily unnerved).

But you have to live, and live this life, no matter how wide it makes you open your eyes in astonishment at every turn.

The day after this night, basically a wedding night, a canoe was dug out of a tree trunk and put to sea.

They sailed, avoiding the coasts sown with casinos. Oh, wedding trip beneath the suns, as if in a vastness of space.

And landed the third day in Ethiopia where Andromeda's inconsolable father reigned (I leave you to imagine his joy) . . .

Here's the moral:
Young ladies, let this story serve
To spare some monster misery;
It shows that this one well deserved
To be the happiest of the three.

—Translated by Patricia Terry & Nancy Kline

# NOTES

From *Le Sanglot de la Terre* (1878–1882)
*Funeral March for the Death of the Earth*
Page—24

We are invited to attend the Earth's funeral, not our own. The planet in the light of astronomical fact has shrunk to a fragile personification, detached from the immobile ground under our feet. Imagining the Earth as a corpse necessarily gives the commentator a position of superiority to which readers of the poem readily respond. Thus we may be lulled into accepting the rather grim conclusions partly concealed in the encyclopedic catalogue.

Eden, sketched in the second stanza, existed before man stripped Maya (illusion) of its veils and created Time. In the medieval night dominated by Terror, Famine, and Plague, human progress reached the point of cursing its own creations, and so turned to God. But doubt returned to displace "Justice and Father," leaving only the civilized horrors listed in the fifth stanza. The proudest human achievements were those of Buddha (Sakya) and Jesus, whose sacrifices are now merged, in the anonymity of space, with the equally futile accomplishments of the arts. The tormented history of the Earth has only to fade like a nightmare into silence.

Much of *Le Sanglot de la Terre* is devoted to Laforgue's own attitude toward these revelations. In "L'éclair du Gouffre," for example, cries of revolt and despair lead to a demand that God appear to explain "Why life?" In the silence Laforgue again charges the universe: "Oh! heartless spaces! Just a moment, Stars! I don't want to die! . . ."

From *Les Complaintes* (1882–1883)
*Complaint about a Lady Good and Dead*
Page—30

The last line transforms the poem in retrospect to a benign daydream, even a joke. And yet the "loyal stillborn dream" has its own reality. The double-entendre going to the rescue of the possibly sentimental is characteristic of Heine in his more flippant moments.

*Complaint about a Certain Sunday*
Page—32

Dated July, 1883, from Coblentz, the poem is presumably addressed to "R," but particular regrets and obstinacies are sacrificed to the communication of a mood. This is already an inner monologue similar in effect to those of the free-verse poems. ("She left yesterday. Perhaps I mind? Oh, yes! . . .") The mind drifts on the tedium of Sunday from generalizations to random observations and back again, pauses in the present to watch a sunset, and allows the chain reactions of thought to lead from the sun and the enigmatic confidences of evening to ambiguously demanding eyes which in turn evoke death, casting a chill over the moment "Oh, alone! alone! and so cold!" before returning to the pseudo-consolations of ennui. Madrepores, incidentally, are a form of coral; the line refers to the irreversibility of evolution. The refrain has the same function as the recurrent phrases in *Last Poems*, tying the meditations to a central theme.

*Complaint of the Poet's Foetus*
Page—36

As if it were in answer to Baudelaire's "La Vie antérieure," the poem rejects the mysterious languors of the prenatal state for a frenzy of affirmation. Laforgue's foetus will encounter the "secret douloureux" of life only when it is too late, and the "shadowy skirts" will be an insufficient refuge.

The foetus and the aquarium were among Laforgue's most influential images. The foetus speaks for itself. The aquarium forests here refer to a womb landscape, but they also have specific associations with the gloomy obscurities of the unconscious.

*Complaint of the Moon in the Country*
Page—40

The Moon is not even the subject of this complaint, much less the mysterious kingdom of Pierrot. A good old lady with cotton in her ears could hardly be the object of a cult. The quiet couplets are concerned with the poet himself and the peaceful region of his exile, a village square at night, point of departure for mild recollections of "her." There is some evidence that the lady in question was "R." Only one couplet exhibits the typical Laforgue defense:

> Just last winter—how absurd
> If she took my verses at their word!

The poem is dated July, 1884, from Cassel.

*Complaint of Lord Pierrot*
Page—44

One of the best Complaints introduces Pierrot, and a parody of the famous folk song sets the vigorously anti-intellectual mood. It is not Pierrot but the reader who is whirled and shaken, while the hero, his heart "honest and well-behaved," lights bonfires of imaginary love and juggles with absolutes. He may be led by All (presumably the Unconscious), but his self-esteem can dance circles around the defects of love or the insufficiencies of the cosmos. The melancholy conclusion indicates no loss of pride.

*Another Complaint of Lord Pierrot*
Page—50

Pierrot does not "complain," but takes revenge. His replies, seemingly calculated just to deflect the lady's advances, are far from haphazardly chosen. Each of them, on another level of meaning reinforced by the effect of surprise, is an earnest statement of those dissonant elements which for Laforgue are an inevitable ingredient in the love duet.

The concluding stanza of Eliot's "Portrait of a Lady" begins, "Well, and what if she should die this afternoon, . . . Should die and leave me sitting pen in hand . . ." But his "Conversation galante" is a more specific reprise of "Another Complaint." Here it is the lady who responds to sentimental banalities with chaste prose. Eliot's dialogue is very mild, even tepid, as compared with the Laforgue acidities. "Conversation galante" is like a fragment of conversation overheard by a passer-by; Laforgue's is a complete drama in miniature. The last lines of the poems are nearly identical, but "Another Complaint" concludes in the past tense since Pierrot's victim is quite defunct.

## Complaint about Certain Annoyances
Page—52

The "sunset of Cosmogonies" indicates the poet's down-to-earth resolutions which the following line answers with a summary of the consequences, dryly revising an old cry. But even on the terrestrial plane the best of intentions may be warped by "superesthetic blunders."

## Complaint concerning the Poor Human Body
Page—54

Laforgue's horrified materialism in its most violent form. The style conforms to his disgust, the first stanza in particular being harsh, dissonant, even awkward. The rhymes add only a sardonic emphasis to the rigorously uniform tone. The conclusion is pure negation, with the "Substance" (the non-human universe) holding all the cards.

Laforgue has used the body itself as the subject throughout the poem, indicating distinctions between "his" and "hers" only by the couplets.

## Complaint of the King of Thule
Page—58

The King of Thule is an antidote, although he represents the same revolt against the "viviparous holocausts" of human existence. If his purity places him on the side of the Absolute, his song is the gentle lament of an exile rather than a war cry of nihilistic disgust. The danger to lovers comes not from direct or threatening intervention, but from the siren-like attractiveness of the King, even in his defeat. Laforgue has personified the symbol, the golden goblet, of Goethe's poem, so that it is the king himself who sinks below the sea, faithful to an abstract purity rather than to a love realized and lost.

## Complaint about Forgetting the Dead
Page—62

This complaint, addressed to everyone but Laforgue himself, demonstrates his stylistic evolution since *Le Sanglot de la Terre* in dealing with a familiar subject. Death, no longer an instrument in the hands of a universe seeking revenge, is represented here by a taciturn, non-vindictive gravedigger whose knocking on the door pierces our comfortable banalities. The *frisson* he evokes is genuine, and the delicate, even frivolous construction of the short-line stanzas produces a greater emotional impact than all the sincere vehemence of the earlier book.

## Complaint concerning a Poor Young Man
Page—66

This poem, with the "Complaint of the Outraged Husband," comes closer to the folk-song style than any of the other complaints, both of them being modeled on specific songs. The virtuosity of the rhyme scheme should be noted, as the translation does not do it justice; with very minor variations only four rhymes are used throughout the poem.

## Complaint of the Outraged Husband
Page—72

The "Complaint of the Outraged Husband" is probably the most impersonal poem Laforgue ever wrote, although even here the verbal trickery used to outwit Tradition is characteristic.

*Complaint concerning Melancholy and Literary Debates*
Page—76

If it were necessary to select a single poem to represent Laforgue as the poet of his autobiography, one might justifiably choose the "Complaint concerning Melancholy and Literary Debates." The hour is, of course, twilight, resonant with Angelus bells which, inevitably, do not ring for the poet. The first stanza contains a cluster of inventions among which "angelus" acquires a verbal form. Then, with an admirable nonchalance, a convalescent nag is introduced, companion in tranquil misery. The poet is also convalescent, or at least able to put his symptoms in order and prescribe self-mockery as medicine: "Just twice massaged with running life, and you'll be exorcised." Superiority is not enough—this is the disease. And the stanza beginning "Well, having wept over History . . . " is in retrospect only an accurate statement of the facts.

*Complaint about a Convalescence in May*
Page—80

The drifting thoughts of an invalid, this time quietly resisting all his attempts at order. The monotonous tone, the couplets rhymed but with a "dying fall," and such details as the lady "auscultating" passers-by, convey the languid depression that sets in when one is no longer sick enough to dramatize. "My anguished metaphysical cerebrations / Have faded to domestic complications" is precisely Laforgue's *post-Sanglot de la Terre* motto.

From *L'Imitation de Notre-Dame la Lune* (1885)
*Litanies for the First Quarters of the Moon*
Page—86

The invocation increases in power from the relatively commonplace first couplets, associating the Moon with sleepless nights and Endymion, through references to its dead sterility, mystery, and obsessive if neutral interventions, to a recognition of the lunar deity as the unique source of relief and salvation. The "Litanies for the Last Quarters of the Moon" follow a parallel curve of greater intensity, more emphatically equating the "Eucharist of Arcady" with *Le Neant* or death. The poet Leon-Paul Fargue believes that death is the very identity of Laforgue's moon. But any brief definition must be deceptive; the "sterile eye of suicide" owes its effect to a complex cause, and the word "suicide" itself has multiple meanings. The Moon is a manifestation of the Absolute, offering human and intellectual passions the promise that they will one day attain the peace of extinction. It is also an equivalent for "soul," or at least the triumph of mind over the flesh, and a symbol for woman as chastity incarnate (Madonna and Miss, Diana-Artemis.) As the homeland of art, the lunar sterilities are responsible for an effect which may be futile but is nevertheless an affirmation; the product of Laforgue's tête-á-tête with death was always a greater intensity of life.

*Pierrots*

Pages— 90–103

I. Ezra Pound particularly admired "un air d'hydrocéphale asperge" and Laforgue's use of scientific terminology in general. Laforgue was, indeed, from the very beginning of his career, the first, and perhaps is still the most successful experimenter to use science as an ingredient of poetry.

One other point might be worth mentioning as a clue to the character of Pierrot: the ring which identifies the lunar heroes is embellished with an Egyptian scarab; Hamlet in *Moralités légendaires* is provided with a similar token. Other details reinforce this concrete indication of relationship.

The penultimate stanza humorously asserts the vagabond Pierrots' claim to both terrestrial and lunar nourishment. They exist in a no-man's-land between Earth and Infinity, quite self-sufficient enough to mock either or both of them.

II. The Pierrots, like the Moon, are associated with the idea of death. Their intense awareness of the waiting abyss (remember the lunar password: "We must die!") is almost a definition of their originality. It is certainly a factor determining their attitude toward women. Unlike the forlorn clown of the old pantomime, these Pierrots are conquerors by virtue of their uncompromising disdain. They pretend to understand "all wrong;" what they do understand is the shriveling effect of moonlight on feminine promises. This does not save them from regrets.

Only Laforgue would have risked the two concluding images to suggest the primordial and up-to-date rigidity of Pierrot politeness.

III and IV. These show absolute considerations in action on sentimental battlefields. Although the Pierrots' style is second-rate and stammering with scruples, She, desiring some kind of personal immolation, is irresistibly attracted. The exclamation "For moon!" is necessarily ironic. Pierrot's defense is simply that he can't help his own purity.

V. The Genesis of Pierrot theology describes the origin of the Earth among the random throws of a cosmic dice game by which Mind and Heart are trying to solve the problem of their own existence. But the last three stanzas present a defense of the terrestrial viewpoint, even going so far as to suggest that ours would be the best of all possible globes if we could only look away from the extraneous and abstract conflict above our heads. The proper attitude is a thoroughly stoical *Amen*. (And it's a wise doctor who swallows his own cure.)

*Pierrots (A short but typical scene)*
Page—104

This scene may be "typical," but of Laforgue himself. The tone of the monologue is rather startling after the Pierrot pirouettes, and several passages recall the poet's self-analysis in the "Complaint concerning Melancholy and Literary Debates." Two leitmotif phrases are introduced: "deep purple mourning's my native hue" (literally, local color) and "vae soli," (woe to the solitary) which occurs repeatedly in Ezra Pound's *Pisan Cantos. Personae* contains a spirited translation of this poem.

The "short but typical scene" pretends to be a practical illustration of what happens when an ostensibly sincere man tries to deal with Woman. He admits needing her as a remedy against his solitude, recovers wit enough to contrast her cruel insensitivities with the delicacy of his own soul, but finally submits an obscure fidelity as a claim to forgiveness. Whereupon, drawing a weapon from her arsenal, she eludes him with a not unjustified confusion. Laforgue's stage direction *Exit* might just as well have been *Bis*.

*Pierrot Phrases*
Pages— 108–115

It was the philosophy of his own experience that Laforgue had given to the Pierrots, but they in turn supplied him with the suave competence of a fictive identity. The timid exile, expurgator of literary articles for Augusta, certainly did not live the sophisticated style to which the Pierrots are accustomed. By virtue of a successful illusion, a poet who found it difficult to believe in himself has created an imaginary autobiography far more convincing than the real.

In the sixteen short poems of this series the roles of the poet and his hero seem reversed; Pierrot is now concealed behind Laforgue's facade. The poems themselves have a whimsical elegance quite forbidding to accessory explanations.

I. This poem and the two which follow (not included here) were translated by Hart Crane, whose studies of Laforgue proved the adaptability of the Pierrot spirit to a totally foreign milieu.

IX. Laforgue and Pierrot merge in their mastery of the light touch.

X. Perhaps a memory of the long-ago Marguerite.

XVI. Here, Pierrot speaks more for himself.

*Dialogue before Moonrise*
Page—116

An exercise in Laforguian metaphysics concerning the difficulties of attaching life to the Ideal. The first speaker who would "just as soon live" is confronted by the implication that either the Ideal does not exist or life is not to be equated with truth. This provokes a suicidal ultimatum which is jokingly deflected by an intervention from the Infinite. The resulting agreement that the possible and the inconceivable are necessarily if painfully related is counterbalanced by an attempt to establish a terrestrial *raison d'être*. The opposition will admit only that finite existence satisfies its own needs, leaving life enclosed in a vicious circle with the Ideal still threatening from outside. The decision to "follow the Moon" means a rejection of direct rational investigations for lunar illumination where the possible and the ideal can seem to unite despite the facts of Earth: the light of death perhaps, or art, or simply Laforguian grace.

*Litanies for the Last Quarters of the Moon*
Page—120

A passage from this poem appears significantly in the tale "Salome" during Herod's feast: "Three other clowns represented Idea, the Will, and the Unconscious. Idea chattered incessantly, Will pounded his head against the scenery, and Unconscious made the sweeping gestures of someone who really knows a good deal more than he can say right now. This trinity had, moreover, one and the same refrain: O Canaan, tryst / With the good Abyss! / Our Libraries' / Holy destiny!' They had a roaring success."

Satirizing Flaubert's *grand style* did not prevent Laforgue from including Salome among the heroic worshipers of purity. Similarly, in the dedication to *The Imitation of Our Lady the Moon*, he refers to "la petite Salammbo," removing her, by his adjective, from Flaubert's grandiose context in order that the Priestess of Tanit (Astarte) preside over his own Moon.

From *Des Fleurs de Bonne Volonte* (1883–1886)
*Rigors Like None Other*
Page—126

An example of the delicate sensitivity of Laforgue's mature style. Not one syllable protests too much. The meaning is suggested as powerfully as any Symbolist could wish, by the most unpretentious of means.

Laforgue's geranium image was adopted by T. S. Eliot. In "Rhapsody on a Windy Night" we find midnight shaking the memory "as a madman shakes a dead geranium." And a "sunless dry geranium" occurs later in the same poem (following Eliot's version of Laforgue's "La, voyons, mam'zelle la Lune, / Ne gardons pas ainsi rancune.)"

*Next-to-the-last Word*
Page—128

The cruel themes of Le Sanglot de la Terre at their most whimsical, and none the less caustic for that.

*Sundays* (The sky . . .)
Page—132

The theme of the well-brought-up young ladies glimpsed on their way to church or dreaming behind the drawn curtains of boarding schools is here the source for one of Laforgue's finest poems. The obligatory procession passes by silently, like a pale frieze existing more in limbo than in life. Even the supreme revolt makes scarcely a ripple of interruption. But Laforgue's compassion protests in his own evocation of the impassive elements.

*Albums* (not translated)

In an American edition of Laforgue this detailed vision of the Far West deserves at least a comment, although the poem itself is inferior. The hectic gusto with which Laforgue embraces the "cowboy" spirit as his own is unconvincing, and indeed his sophistications would be, to say the least, an amazing intrusion in that society of "desperados" and pioneers for whom he momentarily wished to "scalp" his European brain.

*Sundays* (They decided . . .)
Page—134

This "Sundays" begins with one of the rare references to Darwin in poetry, and presents, as an example of our species' perfection, an at least apparently enthusiastic picture of human activities at their least intellectual. The reader glides over multiple meanings like the skaters, a souvenir of German afternoons, whose apparition further increases the tempo.

*Le Concile féerique* (1886)
*The Faerie Council*
Page—136

The plot has been outlined in the Introduction, but the violence of Laforgue's dramatic language should perhaps be further emphasized. The play, despite its title, is any thing but *féerique*. The Earth is like a "pot of stew," the moon has all the expressiveness of a "lard bladder" and suffers from "purulent ophthalmia." Everything, from the viewpoint of the Chorus, seems to sprawl in the mud. Love is reduced to the agitations of mucous membranes, and is described as a "hacking to pieces" which I have translated, perhaps too mildly, as "butcheries." Ennui or "universal rape" appear as unhappy alternatives. But the *status quo* is nevertheless exalted, at least in preference to anything outside. The Gentleman without illusions accepts women as better than nothing, while the Lady gloats, knowing her powers too well to care what they are called. And the Chorus rather frenetically insists "That's all there is."

From *Derniers Vers* (1886–1887)
I. *The Coming Winter*
Page—152

Variations on a November theme. Although the poem seems to be exclusively devoted to its description of the season, its effect is the communication of a mood. Through a personalized landacape, the poet wanders among the past, present, and future of his melancholy. The dying Sun lies shivering on his "coat" of yellow broom, abandoned to solitude. The rutted winter roads climb upward in a Don Quixotic struggle. The wind "mauls" the clouds, and the melancholy horns trap the poet in his own "echoing tone."

The first line has a variety of meanings obscured in translation. The blockade used by Napoleon as a weapon against England was called the *blocus continental*. "Messageries" often refers to sea transport, and the word for rising sun, "Levant," implies the geographical Orient. Thus the two phrases are intended to suggest the physical and emotional closing-in of the winter fogs and enforced isolation.

Laforgue as the poet of cities is once again close to the Baudelairean tradition, but he prefers to select only those aspects of metropolitan life which familiarity has rendered banal—woolen clothes, pharmacies, cakes and tea, newspapers. Although a view of rooftops may become an ocean, the "metropolitan wretchedness" never aspires to grandeur. This comprehensive domesticity even touches the metaphysical when Time is discovered knitting slippers!

## II. *The Mystery of the Three Horns*
Page—158

The "mystery" centers on the identity of the horns, and all solutions must remain theoretical since Laforgue has not provided enough clues. Warren Ramsey calls the poem "a little allegory on the fortunes of extroverts and introverts." William Jay Smith reports that the horns represent the heart and the head, while the third member of the party is death in the form of a uniting echo. He also finds associations with various aspects of the Moon.

The information we are offered by the text is as follows: Two horns call to each other, the first blowing so violently that his forehead veins swell; the other, in the woods, is more restrained. The second horn is going to watch the sunset with his "belle," and so eludes his friend in the plain. The phrase "ma belle" is qualified only by the couplet which follows, presumably the voice of the third horn, although it might be interpreted as a further supplication from the plain. In either case the reference to the heroic slaughter at Roncevaux is rather sinister. The most violent of Laforgue's sunsets intervenes. (The river of gold which is mentioned here and also in "The Coming Winter" is the Pactolus, legendary site of Croesus' wealth and the disenchantment of Midas.) Afterward the three horns meet, and go off to have a drink at an inn named for the patron saint of hunters. They apparently kill themselves. The mystery, we are told, is "immoral;" and Laforgue seems to have intended that it be enjoyed from a discreet distance.

III. *Sundays* (To give myself . . .)
Page—164

The point of departure is the old problem of "taking the first step," from which a series of familiar Laforguian themes are unraveled—the cry of V*ae soli* in combat with regrets, the pariah on Sunday, unapproachable young ladies armored by prayerbooks, the desire to force a reconciliation with the facts of life, the repudiation of these same facts (as Pan in the *Moralités* also protests, "It isn't her flesh that would be all for me!"), finally a self-mockery reminiscent of "Just twice massaged with running life . . ." Once communicated via the chaste ironies of Pierrot, these elements of Laforgue's inner self now seem to be offered as a spontaneous and intimate confidence. This illusion, however, belongs exclusively to the reader.

Laforgue's primary concern, to discover the rhythm of emotions and the "music of ideas," has simply transferred the protective irony to a deeper level. No poet was ever more aware of the ambiguities involved in the substitution of art for life, as witness the self-accusations of Hamlet concerning his own truth-revealing play: "Little by little I forgot that it concerned my murdered father, robbed of all that he still had to live in this precious world (poor man, poor man!), my prostituted mother (the vision that wrecked Woman for me and made me drive the celestial Ophelia to die of shame and deterioration); to say nothing of my throne! I went along arm in arm with the fictions of a fine subject. (It is a fine subject, you know!) I did it all over again in iambics; I slipped in extraneous delicacies. . . . And in the evening when I had nailed the last rhyme to some revolutionary tirade, I went to sleep in the innocence of my lily-white conscience, smiling at domesticated chimeras like a good fellow who has only to provide for a large family with his able pen." So Laforgue, too, must keep his secrets.

IV. *Sundays* (It's autumn . . .)
Page—170

The mood has not changed in these "Sundays," where once again the chapel-bound young ladies provoke an attempt to conquer vae soli somewhere out of this world. But an increased generalization, almost impersonality, is noticeable in this poem. The Antigones and Philomelas mingled with the falling leaves anticipate Laforgue's transfer of his own characteristic attitudes to Lohengrin, Salome, Andromeda, and her gentlemanly Dragon in the *Moralités légendaires*. "Sundays" gives the poet himself the titles of Polar Bear for his reticence and Grand Chancellor of Analysis for his pernicious intelligence. So stylized, he offers a longing admiration to the young girl hidden from the everyday world like an "ideal violet" protected by the universe, and yet docilely human enough to need forgiveness (Laforgue's, of course) for her innocently inviting eyelashes. Beyond "conquest" he would promise her escape from the rest of their bored species satiated with its indigestible High Mass, but she?

V. *Petition*
Page—176
Translated for this edition.

"Absolute love" with which the poem begins, is, as usual, only a negative subject. The kind of love available is expressed in the banality of social conversation. In "La Figlia che piange" Eliot translates a significant passage as "as simple and faithless as a smile and a shake of the hand." But neither a smile (not in the text) nor a handshake is inevitably faithless. I prefer to translate "comme un bonjour" as "have a good day"—even though this empty expression, one hopes, will become less ubiquitous in the course of the 21st century.

Laforgue complains that social codes dictate for women a stance of superiority, an "angel rôle" which nevertheless gains her only a degrading marriage. He imagines a more fulfilling relationship of equals, as brother and sister content with each other, at peace—a rare dream for Laforgue.

VI. Simple Agony
Page—182

With "Simple Agony" the pariah mood returns, encouraged now by the sympathies of May to direct itself toward the creation of some "more mortal" world. In this most musically beautiful of all Laforgue's poems, an intricately curved rhythmic pattern rises out of the words as if it were in itself "the thing which is the thing," an antidote for life's brutalities, the animals unjustly beaten, the women "ugly forever." Laforgue would break the world with the very intensity of his human pity, believing that life is at least as cruel as those who live it. In the calmly narrative concluding section "he" dies for love, drawn away from prudence by autumnal horn-calls, killed by a simple accident of being, far from regrets. And Laforgue, having told his story, warns his listeners back to the safety of their homes.

"There's no more REASON," quoted with enthusiasm by Paul Eluard, was a natural slogan for surrealists and dadaists, thanks to an interpretation considerably more literal than Laforgue's. In spite of his emphasis on the "unconscious," and certain intuitions which have been called pre-Freudian ("When I arrange a trip down into Me . . .") Laforgue could only be imagined as a participant in these revolutions by a confusion in terms. Recognition of the essential contribution of irrational elements to poetry is not the same as accepting the subconscious mind as an exclusive source.

VII. *Solo by Moonlight*
Page—188

Laforgue was exiled from love by "spleen," a word that in 1957 I translated "ennui," believing that the imported word in English better communicated the meaning: "melancholia founded on total boredom." But in 2008 I find that definition too confining. Thus I have replaced "ennui" with "bad moods" whenever that was possible.

VIII *Legend*
Page—196
Translation for this edition.

Out of a chaos of words suggestive of religion and illness emerges an indistinct female figure "Fleeing herself the length of the Sea's superhuman cries." She comes close, starts to tell a banal story, laments the approach of bad weather, which, considering her poor health, evokes some sympathy from the narrator. But their conversation quickly degenerates into quarrel-ing, a retreat into the poet's childhood memories, and a final boast of hypo-thetical fidelity.

IX. *Oh! if one of Them . . .*
Page—202

Pierrot's earlier demand for perfect feminine devotion is grandiloquently answered, if only by a dream. The poem's straight-faced enthusiasm is unchallenged except by two quite unobtrusive phrases which nevertheless provide the decisive mockery. When She, having made her way like a flash of lightning through the storms of the world, pauses to wipe her feet before crossing Laforgue's threshold, we are amiably undeceived. The deliberately lengthened line in the last stanza, "And roll on the mat I had just for that purpose put there," once again pricks the dramatic balloon. Another detail of the poem's subtle mechanism is found in the second stanza, where the abstract "I love you" is neatly personified into an irresistible vision of the ideal young lady by the inconspicuous phrase "lowers its eyes."

X *O diaphanous geraniums*
Page—206

The most manic of the Last Poems, beginning with a chaos of words held together only by their sounds and the fascination of their eccentric juxtposi-tions, strong rhythms giving an air of conviction to what is, at most, a vague impression of meaning. There follows a momentary dream of life at peace and at home, which is lost to a nightmare of "improvisation:" attractions, rejections, self-pity, paranoia, heroic stances, love as lode-star, solitude.

XI. *About a Defunct Lady*
Page—210

"About a Defunct Lady" convincingly demonstrates the results of analy-sis plus imagination. Logic reveals the lover's self-delusion. The hypothetical alternatives A, B, C, or D might just as well exist—in a moment they do exist! Once there is a possible rival, the plot escapes from its author, who is drawn, like his readers, into belief. Seeing Her in the arms of another man, what is left but to rush away "across the oncoming autumn" and hide a stone-cold heart at home. But all at once the accumulation of melancholy startles the dreamer into turning on his dream with a furiously protesting "No thanks!"

XII. Black wind . . .
Page—216

The last poem is a summary and a farewell. Preceded by what must have been the most companionable of Laforgue's quotations from *Hamlet*, a dirge invokes the darkest season of a heart so burdened with pity and love that it can look only to the storm outside for solace. Then thoughts of Her occasion feelings of solitude (but unrepentant: "Oh! that misery of wanting to be our wife!") and recommendations for the nunnery, apparently in Tarbes, where ladies committed to virtue "walk forever frozen / With lowered eyes."

The vision demands its own negation. The wind seems suddenly to cry out for compromise, "We must be two beside a fire." But this again is swept aside; She, at least, is not to give in to these "great pities of November." In the end Laforgue prays once more for the courage and strength (Baudelaire's words, softened by humility) to live life's dizzying fair, since "sooner or later we'll be dead."

"Perseus and Andromeda" from *Legends and Morals* (*Moraltés légendaires*)
Tramslated with Nancy Klein.
Page—223

On August 7, 1886, Laforgue wrote to his old friend Gustave Kahn, offering to send him a copy of "*Persée et Andromède*," which he described as "*ravissant—je me suis surpassé! à mon âge!*" His age was twenty-six; almost exactly a year later he would be dead. The tale, from *Moralités Légendaires* is indeed "enchanting" in every sense of the word, and one could certainly agree that he had out-done himself, regardless of his age, having managed, despite tuberculosis and poverty, to reinvent French prose, even as the free verse poems of Derniers Vers were being published. During this otherwise bleak last year of his life, Laforgue had the comfort of faithful, concerned friends, the presence of his wife, Leah Lee, "full of gaiety and whimsy," and took great pleasure in the fact that his works, appearing in Paris journals, were enthusiastically welcomed.

This information comes from letters published in *Oeuvres complètes de Jules Laforgue, L'Age d'homme*, 3 vols., 1995.

Patricia Terry was Professor of French Literature at Barnard College and the University of California San Diego until her retirement in 1991. Among her verse translations are *Poems of Jules Laforgue, The Song of Roland, Poems of the Elder Edda, The Honeysuckle and the Hazel Tree, Renard the Fox,* and *Roof Slates and Other Poems of Pierre Reverdy* (with Mary Ann Caws). Recent titles include *Capital of Pain* by Paul Eluard (with Mary Ann Caws and Nancy Kline), an illustrated edition of *Lancelot and the Lord of Distant Isles: Or, The Book of Galehaut Retold* (with Samuel N. Rosenberg), *The Sea and Other Poems* by Guillevic, and a book of her own poems, *Words of Silence*. At present she is working in collaboration with Samuel N. Rosenberg on a collection of late medieval folk poems from France and Spain, with Nancy Kline on a collection of the poems of Jules Superveille (Black Widow Press 2011), and also with Nancy Kline, volume two of the *Essential Poems and Prose of Jules Laforgue,* comprising the *Moralités légendaires.*

Nancy Kline was founding director of the Writing Program at Barnard College, where she taught in the English and French departments. She has published six books, fiction and nonfiction alike, and has won a National Endowment for the Arts Creative Writing Grant. Her stories, essays, memoirs and reviews have appeared widely.

WWW.BLACKWIDOWPRESS.COM

This book was set in Simoncini Garamond. The titling font is Aculida, a modernistic typeface used by many of the Dadaists in their typographic artworks.

typeset & designed by Windhaven Press
www.windhaven.com

# TITLES FROM BLACK WIDOW PRESS

## TRANSLATION SERIES

*Approximate Man and Other Writings*
by Tristan Tzara. Translated and edited by Mary Ann Caws.

*Art Poétique*
by Guillevic. Translated by Maureen Smith.

*Capital of Pain*
by Paul Eluard. Translated by Mary Ann Caws, Patricia Terry, and Nancy Kline.

*Chanson Dada: Selected Poems*
by Tristan Tzara. Translated with an introduction and essay by Lee Harwood.

*Essential Poems and Writings of Joyce Mansour: A Bilingual Anthology*
Translated with an introduction by Serge Gavronsky.

*Essential Poems and Writings of Robert Desnos: A Bilingual Anthology*
Edited with an introduction and essay by Mary Ann Caws.

*EyeSeas (Les Ziaux)*
by Raymond Queneau. Translated with an introduction by Daniela Hurezanu and Stephen Kessler.

*The Inventor of Love & Other Writings*
by Gherasim Luca. Translated by Julian and Laura Semilian. Introduction by Andrei Codrescu. Essay by Petre Răileanu.

*La Fontaine's Bawdy*
by Jean de la Fontaine. Translated with an introduction by Norman R. Shapiro.

*Last Love Poems of Paul Eluard*
Translated with an introduction by Marilyn Kallet.

*Love, Poetry (L'amour la poésie)*
by Paul Eluard. Translated with an essay by Stuart Kendall.

*Poems of André Breton: A Bilingual Anthology*
Translated with essays by Jean-Pierre Cauvin and Mary Ann Caws.

*Poems of A.O. Barnabooth*
by Valéry Larbaud. Translated by Ron Padgett and Bill Zavatsky.

*Preversities: A Jacques Prévert Sampler*
Translated and edited by Norman R. Shapiro.

*The Sea and Other Poems*
by Guillevic. Translated by Patricia Terry. Introduction by Monique Chefdor.

*To Speak, to Tell You?*
Poems by Sabine Sicaud. Translated by Norman R. Shapiro. Introduction and notes by Odile Ayral-Clause.


## FORTHCOMING TRANSLATIONS

*Essential Poems and Writings of Jules Laforgue*
Translated and edited by Patricia Terry.

*Essential Poems and Writings of Pierre Reverdy*
Translated by Mary Ann Caws and Patricia Terry.

*Furor and Mystery & Other Writings*
by René Char. Edited and translated by Mary Ann Caws and Nancy Kline.

*I Want No Part in It and Other Writings*
by Benjamin Péret. Translated with an introduction by James Brook.

*The Big Game*
by Benjamin Péret. Translated with an introduction by Marilyn Kallet.

*A Life of Poems, Poems of a Life*
by Anna de Noailles. Translated by Norman R. Shapiro. Introduction by Catherine Perry.


## MODERN POETRY SERIES

*An Alchemist with One Eye on Fire*
by Clayton Eshleman.

*Anticline*
by Clayton Eshleman.

*Archaic Design*
by Clayton Eshleman.

*Backscatter: New and Selected Poems*
by John Olson.

*The Caveat Onus*
by Dave Brinks. The complete cycle, four volumes in one.

*Crusader-Woman*
by Ruxandra Cesereanu. Translated by Adam J. Sorkin. Introduction by Andrei Codrescu.

*Fire Exit*
by Robert Kelly.

*Forgiven Submarine*
by Ruxandra Cesereanu and Andrei Codrescu.

*The Grindstone of Rapport: A Clayton Eshleman Reader*
Forty years of poetry, prose, and translations by Clayton Eshleman.

*Packing Light: New and Selected Poems*
by Marilyn Kallet.

*Signal from Draco: New and Selected Poems*
by Mebane Robertson.


## Forthcoming Modern Poetry Titles

*Concealments and Caprichos*
by Jerome Rothenberg.

*Curdled Skulls: Poems of Bernard Bador*
Translated by Clayton Eshleman and Bernard Bador.

*from stone this running*
by Heller Levinson.

*Larynx Galaxy*
by John Olson.

*Present Tense of the World: Poems 2000–2008*
by Amina Saïd. Translated by Marilyn Hacker.

*Exile is My Trade: A Habib Tengour Reader*
Translated by Pierre Joris.


## LITERARY THEORY / BIOGRAPHY SERIES

*Revolution of the Mind: The Life of André Breton*
by Mark Polizzotti. Revised and augmented edition.


# www.blackwidowpress.com